LOGAN XANDER

3D Game Programming

Mastering 3D Development Techniques for Dynamic Gaming Experience

First edition

This book was professionally typeset on Reedsy.
Find out more at reedsy.com

Contents

Introduction

Overview of 3D Game Development

3D game development is a multi-faceted process that combines artistry, technology, and storytelling to create immersive interactive experiences. In recent years, the gaming industry has seen exponential growth, with 3D games leading the charge due to their enhanced visual appeal and engaging gameplay mechanics. Unlike 2D games, which limit players to a flat surface, 3D games provide depth and realism that allows for more complex environments, characters, and interactions. This shift toward three-dimensional graphics has opened the doors to limitless creative possibilities, attracting a diverse audience ranging from casual gamers to dedicated enthusiasts.

The process of developing a 3D game typically involves several stages, including conceptualization, design, programming, testing, and deployment. During the conceptualization phase, developers brainstorm ideas and create a game design document (GDD) that outlines the game's core mechanics, story, and visual style. Once the concept is solidified, artists and designers work on creating the game's assets, such as characters, environments, and animations. Programmers then bring these assets to life, coding the game mechanics and integrating them into a cohesive experience.

3D game development is often facilitated by the use of specialized software tools, known as game engines. These engines provide a framework for building games, offering functionalities such as rendering graphics, simulating physics, and managing user inputs. Popular game engines like Unity and Unreal Engine have democratized game development, allowing both seasoned developers and newcomers to create high-quality games with relative ease.

Why 3D Games?

The appeal of 3D games lies in their ability to immerse players in richly detailed virtual worlds that simulate real-life environments. This level of immersion is achieved through advanced graphics, sound design, and gameplay mechanics that engage the senses and evoke emotional responses. Players can navigate complex landscapes, interact with lifelike characters, and experience narratives that unfold in dynamic ways, making 3D games not only visually stimulating but also intellectually and emotionally engaging.

Furthermore, the rise of virtual reality (VR) and augmented reality (AR) technologies has propelled 3D gaming into new dimensions. These technologies provide players with an unprecedented level of interactivity and presence, allowing them to physically move within the game space and interact with virtual objects as if they were real. This evolution in gaming technology is reshaping how games are designed, pushing developers to innovate and create experiences that were once thought impossible.

The increasing popularity of 3D games can also be attributed to their versatility. From action-packed shooters and role-playing games to simulation and educational titles, the 3D format can cater to various genres and audiences. Developers can experiment with gameplay mechanics, art styles, and storytelling techniques, resulting in a diverse array of games that appeal to different tastes and preferences.

Moreover, the commercial success of 3D games has attracted significant investment in the gaming industry. Major gaming companies and independent developers alike are capitalizing on the demand for 3D experiences, leading to a flourishing market that offers both opportunities for innovation and challenges in a competitive landscape. The economic potential of 3D gaming continues to expand, with the global gaming market projected to reach hundreds of billions of dollars in the coming years.

Understanding 3D Game Engines

At the heart of 3D game development is the game engine, a software framework that streamlines the development process by providing essential tools and features. Game engines are designed to handle various aspects of game creation, including rendering graphics, managing physics, and supporting audio. They serve as the backbone of a game, allowing developers to focus on creating engaging content without needing to build everything from scratch.

Popular game engines like Unity and Unreal Engine each have unique strengths that cater to different development needs. Unity is renowned for its user-friendly interface, extensive asset store, and versatility, making it an excellent choice for both 2D and 3D games. Its support for C# programming and a strong community of developers make it accessible to newcomers while still offering advanced features for seasoned professionals.

Unreal Engine, on the other hand, is celebrated for its high-fidelity graphics and robust capabilities for large-scale projects. Utilizing C++ programming, it provides developers with fine-grained control over performance and graphical fidelity. Unreal Engine is often the preferred choice for AAA game development due to its advanced rendering capabilities, particularly in creating realistic environments and character models.

Choosing the right game engine depends on the specific requirements of the project, including the desired visual style, target platform, and team expertise. Understanding the strengths and limitations of each engine is crucial for making informed decisions during the development process.

Tools and Software Needed

In addition to game engines, a variety of tools and software are essential for successful 3D game development. Artists, programmers, and designers must collaborate using specialized applications tailored to their roles. Below are some key categories of tools necessary for creating a 3D game:

1. Modeling Software:

- **Blender:** A free and open-source 3D modeling tool that allows users to create, animate, and render 3D models. It's favored for its versatility and powerful features.
- **Maya:** A professional-grade software used for character rigging, animation, and modeling, widely recognized in the film and gaming industries.

2. Texturing and Materials:

- **Substance Painter:** A texturing tool that enables artists to create realistic textures for 3D models, providing an intuitive interface and extensive material libraries.
- **Photoshop:** While primarily a 2D graphics editor, Photoshop is often used for creating textures and UI elements in game development.

3. Animation Software:

- **3ds Max:** Known for its powerful animation and rigging tools, it's a popular choice among game developers for character animation.
- **Mixamo:** An online platform offering a library of animated character rigs that can be easily integrated into game engines.

4. Sound Design:

- **Audacity:** A free audio editing tool that allows developers to record, edit, and manipulate sound effects and music for games.
- **FMOD:** A widely-used audio middleware that enables dynamic audio implementation, providing developers with control over sound design.

5. Version Control:

- **Git:** A version control system that allows teams to manage code changes efficiently. It's essential for collaborative projects to ensure everyone is working on the latest version of the game.

6. Integrated Development Environments (IDEs):

- **Visual Studio:** A popular IDE for C# and C++ programming that integrates seamlessly with Unity and Unreal Engine, facilitating efficient coding and debugging.

These tools and software are integral to the game development pipeline, allowing teams to collaborate effectively and produce high-quality games.

How to Use This Book

This book is designed to be a comprehensive guide for anyone interested in delving into the world of 3D game development. Whether you're a complete novice or an experienced developer looking to refine your skills, the following sections will equip you with the knowledge and tools necessary to succeed.

Structure of the Book:

Each chapter focuses on a specific aspect of 3D game development, offering detailed explanations, practical examples, and hands-on exercises to reinforce learning. The chapters are structured to build upon one another, gradually guiding you through the development process from initial concept to final deployment.

Key Features:

- **Practical Exercises:** Each chapter includes exercises designed to apply the concepts learned, helping you build a portfolio of projects as you progress through the book.
- **Resources and References:** Additional resources, including online tutorials, forums, and asset libraries, are provided at the end of each chapter to further enhance your learning experience.
- **Project-Based Approach:** Throughout the book, you'll work on a sample game project, allowing you to see how theoretical concepts translate into real-world development practices.

Tips for Success:

- **Practice Regularly:** The best way to learn game development is through hands-on practice. Experiment with the tools and techniques discussed in each chapter.
- **Join the Community:** Engaging with online communities and forums can provide valuable insights, feedback, and support as you navigate your game development journey.
- **Stay Curious:** The gaming industry is constantly evolving. Stay updated on the latest trends, technologies, and best practices to keep your skills relevant.

By following this guide, you will gain a solid foundation in 3D game development, empowering you to create captivating games that engage players and showcase your creativity. Welcome to the exciting world of 3D game development—let's get started!

Chapter 1: Introduction to Game Design

Game Mechanics and Concepts

G ame mechanics are the rules and systems that govern gameplay, shaping how players interact with the game world and achieve their objectives. Understanding game mechanics is essential for designing engaging and balanced games. These mechanics can be categorized into several core concepts:

1. Core Mechanics

Core mechanics refer to the fundamental actions that players can take within a game. These mechanics form the backbone of gameplay and define how players engage with the game. Common core mechanics include:

- **Movement:** How characters navigate the game world, whether through walking, running, jumping, or flying.
- **Combat:** The systems governing how players engage in fights, including attack, defense, and special abilities.
- **Resource Management:** The mechanics of collecting, spending, and managing resources such as health, ammunition, and currency.
- **Puzzle Solving:** Mechanics that require players to solve challenges or riddles using logic, pattern recognition, or exploration.

2. Game Objectives

Objectives give players a sense of purpose and direction within the game. They can range from simple tasks to complex missions and often involve goals like reaching a specific location, defeating a certain number of enemies, or solving puzzles. Objectives can be classified into:

- **Primary Objectives:** The main goals that drive the game's narrative and progress the player through the story.
- **Secondary Objectives:** Optional tasks that provide rewards or enhance gameplay but are not necessary to complete the main story.
- **Long-Term Objectives:** Goals that span across multiple play sessions, encouraging players to invest time into the game.

3. Feedback Systems

Feedback systems provide players with information about their actions and progress in the game. Effective feedback helps players understand the consequences of their decisions, guiding them to improve their gameplay. Common feedback methods include:

- **Visual Feedback:** Changes in the game world, such as animations, effects, or UI updates that indicate player actions or state changes.
- **Audio Feedback:** Sound effects and music that respond to player actions, reinforcing gameplay mechanics and emotional engagement.
- **Progress Indicators:** Systems such as health bars, score counters, and achievement notifications that keep players informed about their status and accomplishments.

4. Balancing Mechanics

Balancing mechanics is crucial for creating a fair and engaging gameplay experience. Developers must consider the interactions between various mechanics to ensure no single aspect overpowers others. Common balancing techniques include:

- **Difficulty Scaling:** Adjusting the game's challenge based on player skill level or progress to maintain engagement.
- **Playtesting:** Gathering feedback from players to identify and rectify imbalances in gameplay, ensuring a smooth experience for diverse audiences.
- **Iterative Design:** Continuously refining mechanics based on testing and feedback to improve the overall gameplay experience.

Understanding these mechanics is vital for creating a game that is enjoyable, challenging, and accessible to players. By mastering core concepts, developers can design gameplay experiences that captivate and retain audiences.

Genres of 3D Games

3D games span a wide array of genres, each with distinct gameplay styles, themes, and mechanics. Recognizing these genres is essential for understanding player expectations and designing games that meet them. Below are some of the most popular genres of 3D games:

1. Action Games

Action games focus on fast-paced gameplay that emphasizes physical challenges and hand-eye coordination. Players often engage in combat and navigate dynamic environments filled with obstacles and enemies. Key sub-genres include:

- **Platformers:** Players control characters that jump between platforms and navigate levels, often with a focus on timing and precision (e.g., *Super Mario Odyssey*).
- **Shooter Games:** These games center on shooting mechanics, with players typically controlling a character armed with weapons. Sub-genres include first-person shooters (FPS) and third-person shooters (TPS) (e.g., *Call of Duty* and *Gears of War*).

2. Adventure Games

Adventure games prioritize storytelling and exploration over combat and action. Players often solve puzzles, interact with characters, and uncover narrative elements. Sub-genres include:

- **Graphic Adventures:** Games that rely heavily on visual storytelling and player choices, often featuring intricate narratives (e.g., *Life is Strange*).
- **Action-Adventure:** A blend of action and adventure elements, combining exploration with combat and puzzle-solving (e.g., *The Legend of Zelda: Breath of the Wild*).

3. Role-Playing Games (RPGs)

RPGs allow players to assume the roles of characters in a fictional world, often featuring character customization, skill progression, and narrative depth. Key types of RPGs include:

- **Traditional RPGs:** Players navigate a story-driven world, complete quests, and develop characters through experience points and skill trees (e.g., *Final Fantasy VII*).
- **Massively Multiplayer Online RPGs (MMORPGs):** Online games that allow thousands of players to interact in a shared world, engaging in quests, trading, and combat (e.g., *World of Warcraft*).

4. Simulation Games

Simulation games aim to replicate real-world activities and systems, allowing players to experiment and explore in a controlled environment. Popular sub-genres include:

- **Life Simulation:** Games that simulate aspects of life, such as building relationships and managing daily tasks (e.g., *The Sims*).
- **Vehicle Simulation:** Games that focus on driving, flying, or piloting vehicles, offering realistic experiences and mechanics (e.g., *Microsoft Flight Simulator*).

5. Strategy Games

Strategy games require players to plan and make tactical decisions to achieve victory. They often emphasize resource management, unit control, and strategic thinking. Sub-genres include:

- **Real-Time Strategy (RTS):** Players control units and resources in real-time, requiring quick decision-making (e.g., *StarCraft II*).
- **Turn-Based Strategy (TBS):** Players take turns to make decisions and move units, allowing for deeper strategic planning (e.g., *Civilization VI*).

6. Horror Games

Horror games aim to evoke fear and tension through atmosphere, narrative, and gameplay mechanics. They often incorporate survival elements, limited resources, and psychological themes (e.g., *Resident Evil* and *Amnesia: The Dark Descent*).

Each genre presents unique challenges and opportunities for game designers. Understanding these genres allows developers to target specific audiences and create experiences that resonate with players.

The Game Development Pipeline

The game development pipeline is a structured process that guides developers from the initial concept of a game to its final release. This pipeline typically includes several key phases, each contributing to the overall development of the game. Below is a breakdown of the stages involved in the game development pipeline:

1. Concept and Pre-Production

The initial phase involves brainstorming and conceptualizing the game idea. Developers outline the game's vision, defining core mechanics, story elements, and visual style. Key activities include:

- **Game Design Document (GDD):** A comprehensive document that outlines the game's objectives, mechanics, art style, and narrative. The GDD serves as a roadmap for the development team throughout the project.
- **Prototype Development:** Creating a basic version of the game to test ideas and mechanics. Prototyping helps identify potential issues early in the development process and allows for adjustments before full production begins.

2. Production

The production phase is where most of the game development occurs. Teams work collaboratively to create assets, implement mechanics, and build the game world. This stage includes:

- **Art and Asset Creation:** Artists design and produce visual elements, including characters, environments, animations, and user interfaces.
- **Programming:** Developers write the code that drives game mechanics, AI behavior, and user interactions. This is often an iterative process,

involving constant testing and refinement.

- **Sound Design:** Sound designers create audio assets, including sound effects, voice acting, and music, enhancing the game's atmosphere and emotional impact.

3. Testing

Testing is a critical phase that ensures the game is polished and free of bugs. This phase typically involves several types of testing:

- **Quality Assurance (QA) Testing:** QA teams playtest the game extensively, identifying bugs, glitches, and gameplay imbalances. This feedback is crucial for refining the game before release.
- **User Testing:** Developers gather feedback from external players to assess usability and overall enjoyment. This testing can provide valuable insights into how the game resonates with the target audience.

4. Polishing

Once testing is complete, developers enter the polishing phase. This involves refining gameplay, fixing bugs, and optimizing performance. Key activities include:

- **Balancing Gameplay:** Developers adjust mechanics and difficulty levels to ensure a satisfying experience for players.
- **Finalizing Assets:** Artists and sound designers complete any outstanding visual or audio elements, ensuring they meet the desired quality standards.

5. Release

The release phase marks the culmination of the development process. Developers prepare for the launch of the game, which may involve:

- **Marketing and Promotion:** Creating promotional materials, trailers, and social media campaigns to generate interest in the game prior to launch.
- **Distribution:** Deciding on the platforms for release (e.g., PC, console, mobile) and preparing for distribution through online stores and physical retailers.

6. Post-Release Support

Following the game's launch, developers may continue to support the title through updates, patches, and downloadable content (DLC). This phase involves:

- **Community Engagement:** Interacting with players through forums and social media to gather feedback and address concerns.
- **Updates and Expansions:** Developers may release patches to fix bugs or introduce new content, ensuring the game remains relevant and enjoyable for players.

Understanding the game development pipeline is crucial for aspiring game developers. By following a structured approach, teams can efficiently manage their projects and deliver high-quality games to players.

Storytelling in 3D Games

Storytelling is a fundamental aspect of 3D game design, enriching the gameplay experience and engaging players on an emotional level. Effective storytelling in games involves weaving narrative elements seamlessly into gameplay, allowing players to experience the story through their actions and decisions. Key components of storytelling in 3D games include:

1. Narrative Structure

The narrative structure of a game determines how the story unfolds. Common narrative structures in 3D games include:

- **Linear Narratives:** The story progresses in a fixed sequence, guiding players through a predetermined path (e.g., many single-player RPGs).
- **Branching Narratives:** Players' choices affect the story, leading to multiple outcomes and endings. This structure enhances replayability and player agency (e.g., *The Witcher 3: Wild Hunt*).

2. Character Development

Strong characters are essential for engaging storytelling. Developers must create relatable and compelling characters that players can connect with emotionally. Key aspects of character development include:

- **Backstory:** Providing characters with rich histories and motivations helps players understand their actions and choices.
- **Character Arcs:** Characters should undergo growth or change throughout the game, reflecting the impact of player choices and narrative events.

3. World-Building

The game world serves as a backdrop for the story, influencing the narrative and player experience. Effective world-building includes:

- **Lore and History:** Developing a rich history for the game world, complete with myths, legends, and conflicts, adds depth to the narrative.
- **Environmental Storytelling:** Using the game environment to con-

vey story elements, such as abandoned buildings or hidden artifacts, encourages exploration and discovery.

4. Player Agency

Player agency allows individuals to make meaningful choices that influence the story. By providing options and consequences, developers empower players to shape the narrative according to their preferences. Key methods for enhancing player agency include:

- **Dialogue Choices:** Allowing players to choose how their character responds in conversations can significantly impact relationships and story outcomes.
- **Moral Dilemmas:** Presenting players with tough choices forces them to consider the consequences of their actions, adding emotional weight to the narrative.

5. Immersive Storytelling Techniques

Developers can employ various techniques to enhance storytelling in 3D games, including:

- **Cutscenes:** Cinematic sequences that advance the narrative while providing a break from gameplay. Well-crafted cutscenes can evoke strong emotions and deepen players' connections to the story.
- **In-Game Events:** Integrating narrative elements into gameplay through scripted events or dynamic interactions helps maintain immersion and keeps players engaged.

6. Emotional Engagement

Ultimately, the goal of storytelling in 3D games is to evoke emotional responses from players. By creating relatable characters, impactful narratives, and immersive experiences, developers can foster a strong connection between players and the game world.

In conclusion, effective storytelling in 3D games involves a careful balance of narrative structure, character development, world-building, and player agency. By mastering these elements, developers can create compelling and memorable experiences that resonate with players long after they have finished the game. Understanding the intricacies of game design lays the foundation for crafting engaging and innovative 3D games, inviting players to embark on unforgettable journeys in virtual worlds.

Chapter 2: Understanding 3D Graphics

2D vs 3D: Key Differences

The distinction between 2D and 3D graphics is fundamental in the field of game design and computer graphics. Understanding these differences is crucial for developers, artists, and designers working in the realm of 3D game development.

1. Dimensionality

The most apparent difference between 2D and 3D graphics lies in their dimensionality.

- **2D Graphics**: These graphics are flat and only have two dimensions—width and height. They are represented on a plane, with images constructed using pixels arranged in a grid. 2D graphics do not convey depth; they lack the ability to depict how objects exist in a three-dimensional space. Common examples include sprites used in 2D platformers, pixel art, and traditional animation.
- **3D Graphics**: In contrast, 3D graphics encompass three dimensions—width, height, and depth. This allows for a more realistic representation of objects and environments. 3D models are created using vertices, edges, and faces, which together form polygons. This dimensionality enables depth perception, allowing players to navigate and interact with

complex environments.

2. Rendering Techniques

Rendering is the process of generating an image from a model by means of computer programs. The rendering techniques differ significantly between 2D and 3D graphics.

- **2D Rendering**: In 2D graphics, rendering is relatively straightforward. Images are drawn directly onto the screen without the need for depth calculations. The rendering pipeline is less complex, as the engine can simply project the 2D images onto the screen. Techniques such as layering, transparency, and sprites are commonly used to create visually appealing effects.
- **3D Rendering**: The rendering process in 3D graphics is more complex and involves multiple steps. 3D models must be transformed from their local coordinates to world coordinates, then to camera coordinates, and finally to screen coordinates. The rendering pipeline in 3D graphics typically includes stages such as modeling, texturing, lighting, and shading. This complexity allows for realistic lighting effects, shadows, and reflections, greatly enhancing the visual fidelity of 3D games.

3. Interactivity

The level of interactivity in games also differs between 2D and 3D environments.

- **2D Interactivity**: In 2D games, player interaction is often limited to moving a character along two axes (left/right, up/down). The game mechanics typically revolve around simple tasks, such as collecting items, jumping, or shooting.
- **3D Interactivity**: In 3D games, players can move freely in a three-dimensional space, allowing for more complex interactions. Players can

explore environments, manipulate objects, and engage in immersive experiences. This interactivity requires more sophisticated game mechanics and design considerations, as developers must account for depth and spatial awareness.

4. Visual Style

The visual style of 2D and 3D graphics can also vary significantly.

- **2D Art Style**: 2D graphics often feature stylized art that emphasizes color, shape, and contrast. Artists can create unique visual experiences through techniques like pixel art, hand-drawn animations, and vector illustrations.
- **3D Art Style**: 3D graphics allow for a more realistic portrayal of characters and environments. However, they can also adopt stylized approaches. Artists can create detailed textures, realistic lighting, and intricate animations, resulting in visually stunning experiences that can range from hyper-realistic to cartoonish.

Understanding these key differences between 2D and 3D graphics lays the foundation for comprehending the complexities involved in 3D game development. Developers and designers must leverage these distinctions to create engaging, interactive, and visually captivating experiences.

Basic Geometry in 3D (Points, Vectors, and Polygons)

Geometry is fundamental to understanding 3D graphics. The basic building blocks of 3D models—points, vectors, and polygons—are essential concepts that developers and artists must grasp to create compelling 3D environments and characters.

1. Points

In 3D graphics, a point is defined by three coordinates in space, representing its position in a three-dimensional coordinate system. The notation typically follows the Cartesian coordinate system (x, y, z), where:

- **X-axis**: Represents the width (left/right) of the object.
- **Y-axis**: Represents the height (up/down) of the object.
- **Z-axis**: Represents the depth (forward/backward) of the object.

Points are the simplest form of representation in 3D graphics and serve as the foundation for creating more complex structures. A single point does not have any dimensions; it simply marks a location in space.

2. Vectors

Vectors are mathematical entities that have both magnitude and direction. In the context of 3D graphics, vectors are crucial for representing various elements, such as movement, force, and orientation. A vector in 3D space is often represented as:

v=(vx,vy,vz)\mathbf{v} = (v_x, v_y, v_z)v=(vx,vy,vz)

Where vxv_xvx, vyv_yvy, and vzv_zvz are the components of the vector along the X, Y, and Z axes, respectively.

Types of Vectors in 3D Graphics:

- **Position Vectors**: Represent the location of a point in space, originating from the origin (0, 0, 0) to the point's coordinates.
- **Direction Vectors**: Indicate a specific direction without considering position. They are often used to represent the direction of movement or a normal to a surface.
- **Normal Vectors**: Perpendicular to a surface, normal vectors are essential in lighting calculations. They define how light interacts with surfaces, affecting shading and reflections.

3. Polygons

Polygons are the fundamental building blocks of 3D models. A polygon is a flat, two-dimensional shape that consists of vertices connected by edges. In 3D graphics, polygons are typically triangular or quadrilateral (quads), with triangles being the most common due to their simplicity and computational efficiency.

Key Properties of Polygons:

- **Vertices**: The points where edges meet. Each vertex has its coordinates in 3D space.
- **Edges**: The lines connecting vertices. Each edge defines a boundary of the polygon.
- **Faces**: The flat surfaces enclosed by edges. In 3D modeling, polygons are often referred to as faces.

Polygons are used to create complex 3D shapes by combining multiple polygons to form a mesh. The process of creating a 3D model typically involves defining the vertices, connecting them to form edges, and enclosing them to create faces.

4. Mesh Structures

A mesh is a collection of vertices, edges, and faces that define the shape of a 3D object in space. Meshes can be simple, like a cube, or highly complex, like a character model.

Types of Meshes:

- **Triangular Meshes**: Composed solely of triangles, these are the most commonly used in real-time rendering due to their efficiency in calculations.
- **Quad Meshes**: Composed of quadrilaterals, these are often used in modeling and animation but may require conversion to triangles for

rendering.

Understanding the basics of geometry—points, vectors, and polygons—is essential for anyone looking to create and manipulate 3D graphics. These concepts provide the foundation for more advanced topics in 3D modeling and rendering.

Coordinate Systems: Cartesian Coordinates

Coordinate systems are fundamental in 3D graphics, as they provide a framework for representing the position and orientation of objects in space. The most commonly used coordinate system in 3D graphics is the Cartesian coordinate system.

1. Cartesian Coordinate System

The Cartesian coordinate system uses three perpendicular axes (X, Y, and Z) to define the position of points in space. The intersection of these axes is known as the origin, represented as (0, 0, 0).
Axes Orientation:

- **X-axis**: Typically runs horizontally, representing left and right.
- **Y-axis**: Runs vertically, representing up and down.
- **Z-axis**: Runs perpendicularly to both the X and Y axes, representing depth (forward and backward).

2. Understanding the Axes

Each axis serves a specific purpose in representing an object's position:

- **X-axis**: Moving along the X-axis changes the position horizontally. Positive values move right, while negative values move left.
- **Y-axis**: Moving along the Y-axis changes the position vertically. Positive

values move upward, while negative values move downward.

- **Z-axis**: Moving along the Z-axis changes the position in depth. Positive values move forward, while negative values move backward.

3. Working with Coordinates

In 3D graphics, every point in space can be described using a set of coordinates (x, y, z). For example, the point (2, 3, -1) indicates a location two units to the right, three units up, and one unit back in the Z direction from the origin.

4. Transformation Matrices

Transformation matrices are used to manipulate objects in 3D space, allowing developers to translate, rotate, and scale models. These matrices operate on the coordinates of points and can be combined to achieve complex transformations.

- **Translation Matrix**: Moves an object from one position to another by adding a specific offset to the coordinates.

$$\begin{pmatrix} 1 & 0 & 0 & t_x \\ 0 & 1 & 0 & t_y \\ 0 & 0 & 1 & t_z \\ 0 & 0 & 0 & 1 \end{pmatrix}$$

Where t_x, t_y, and t_z are the translations along the X, Y, and Z axes, respectively.

- **Rotation Matrix**: Rotates an object around a specified axis by a given angle.

For example, the rotation around the Z-axis can be represented as:

$$\begin{pmatrix} \cos(\theta) & -\sin(\theta) & 0 & 0 \\ \sin(\theta) & \cos(\theta) & 0 & 0 \\ 0 & 0 & 1 & 0 \\ 0 & 0 & 0 & 1 \end{pmatrix}$$

- **Scaling Matrix**: Changes the size of an object by multiplying its coordinates by scale factors.

(sx0000sy0000sz00001)\begin{pmatrix} sx & 0 & 0 & 0 \\ 0 & sy & 0 & 0 \\ 0 & 0 & sz & 0 \\ 0 & 0 & 0 & 1 \end{pmatrix}sx0000sy0000sz00001

Where $sx sxsx$, $sy sysy$, and $sz szsz$ are the scaling factors along the X, Y, and Z axes, respectively.

5. World Space vs. Local Space

In 3D graphics, it's important to differentiate between world space and local space.

- **World Space**: Refers to the global coordinate system in which all objects are positioned. In world space, objects are placed relative to each other within the entire scene.
- **Local Space**: Refers to the coordinate system relative to an individual object. Each object has its own local space, where its origin is typically at its center. Transformations applied in local space affect the object without impacting its position in world space.

Understanding coordinate systems is essential for navigating and manipulating 3D environments. By grasping how objects are positioned and transformed within a three-dimensional space, developers can create dynamic and interactive experiences.

Rendering: The Basics of How 3D Graphics Work

Rendering is the process of generating a visual representation of a 3D scene from a given viewpoint. It involves various stages that translate the abstract representation of a 3D model into a 2D image that can be displayed on a screen. Understanding the basics of rendering is crucial for anyone involved in 3D graphics, as it directly affects the visual quality and performance of a game.

1. The Rendering Pipeline

The rendering pipeline consists of a series of steps that transform 3D models into a 2D image. Each step in the pipeline contributes to the final appearance of the scene. The basic stages of the rendering pipeline include:

- **Modeling**: The creation of 3D models using points, vectors, and polygons, as previously discussed. This step involves defining the geometry and structure of objects in the scene.
- **Texturing**: Applying surface textures to 3D models. Textures add color, detail, and realism to the surfaces of objects. This process involves mapping 2D images onto the 3D surfaces, a technique known as texture mapping.
- **Lighting**: The simulation of light interactions within the scene. Lighting is critical for establishing mood, depth, and realism. Various types of lights (ambient, directional, point, and spotlights) can be used to illuminate the scene and affect how surfaces appear.
- **Shading**: The process of calculating the color and brightness of surfaces based on lighting conditions and material properties. Shading models determine how light interacts with surfaces and can create various effects, such as shadows, reflections, and highlights.
- **Rasterization**: The conversion of 3D data into a 2D image. During rasterization, the 3D models are projected onto a 2D plane (the screen) while preserving their depth information. This stage involves determining which polygons are visible and in what order they should be rendered.
- **Post-Processing**: Additional effects applied to the rendered image to enhance visual quality. Common post-processing techniques include bloom (creating a glow effect), depth of field (blurring distant objects), and anti-aliasing (smoothing jagged edges).

2. Rendering Techniques

Different rendering techniques can be employed to achieve varying levels of visual fidelity and performance. Two primary rendering techniques are:

- **Real-Time Rendering**: Used in video games and interactive applications, real-time rendering aims to generate frames quickly enough to create a seamless experience. Optimizations are crucial in real-time rendering to ensure smooth performance, especially in fast-paced games.
- **Pre-Rendered Graphics**: Used in cinematic scenes or non-interactive content, pre-rendered graphics are generated ahead of time and stored as images or videos. This approach allows for high-quality visuals without the need for real-time calculations, but it sacrifices interactivity.

3. Graphics APIs

Graphics Application Programming Interfaces (APIs) provide developers with the tools to interact with the graphics hardware of a computer. Popular graphics APIs include:

- **OpenGL**: A cross-platform graphics API used for rendering 2D and 3D graphics. It provides developers with a rich set of functions for managing rendering operations.
- **DirectX**: A collection of APIs developed by Microsoft for game development on Windows platforms. Direct3D, a subset of DirectX, is specifically designed for rendering 3D graphics.
- **Vulkan**: A low-level graphics API that provides developers with greater control over GPU resources, allowing for optimized rendering performance.

4. Performance Considerations

Rendering 3D graphics can be computationally intensive, and developers must consider performance optimization to ensure smooth gameplay. Key performance considerations include:

- **Level of Detail (LOD)**: Techniques that reduce the complexity of 3D models when they are farther away from the camera. Lowering the level of detail for distant objects reduces the rendering workload while maintaining visual quality.
- **Culling**: The process of excluding objects that are not visible to the camera from rendering calculations. Techniques such as frustum culling (removing objects outside the camera's view) and occlusion culling (removing objects blocked by other objects) help improve performance.
- **Batching**: Grouping multiple objects together to minimize draw calls to the GPU. Reducing the number of draw calls can significantly enhance rendering performance.

5. Realism and Visual Effects

Achieving realism in 3D graphics often involves implementing various techniques to simulate real-world phenomena. Some common techniques include:

- **Ray Tracing**: A rendering technique that simulates the way light interacts with surfaces by tracing rays of light as they travel through the scene. Ray tracing produces highly realistic images with accurate reflections, refractions, and shadows.
- **Global Illumination**: A technique that accounts for the way light bounces off surfaces and interacts with the environment. Global illumination models the indirect lighting that occurs when light reflects off surfaces, creating more realistic lighting conditions.
- **Particle Systems**: Used to simulate complex phenomena such as fire,

smoke, rain, and explosions. Particle systems generate large numbers of small particles, each with its own properties, to create visually stunning effects.

Understanding the basics of rendering is essential for creating visually compelling 3D games. By mastering the rendering pipeline, techniques, and performance considerations, developers can produce high-quality graphics that enhance the overall gaming experience.

Chapter 3: Exploring 3D Engines

Overview of Popular 3D Engines: Unity, Unreal, Three.js

T he choice of a 3D engine can significantly influence the development process and the final product in game development. Each engine has its unique strengths and weaknesses, catering to different types of projects and developer expertise. In this chapter, we will explore three popular 3D engines: Unity, Unreal Engine, and Three.js.

1. Unity

Unity is one of the most widely used game engines in the world, renowned for its versatility and user-friendly interface. It supports both 2D and 3D game development, making it a popular choice for developers across various genres.

Key Features of Unity:

- **Cross-Platform Support**: Unity allows developers to create games for multiple platforms, including Windows, macOS, Android, iOS, PlayStation, Xbox, and even web browsers.
- **Asset Store**: Unity's Asset Store offers a vast library of pre-built assets, tools, and plugins, enabling developers to speed up their projects and enhance their games.
- **Visual Scripting**: Unity includes a visual scripting tool called Bolt,

which allows developers to create game mechanics without extensive coding knowledge. This feature makes it more accessible for beginners and non-programmers.

- **Extensive Documentation and Community Support**: Unity boasts comprehensive documentation and a large community, providing tutorials, forums, and resources that help developers troubleshoot and learn.

2. Unreal Engine

Unreal Engine is another leading game engine, known for its high-fidelity graphics and advanced capabilities. It is particularly favored in AAA game development due to its robust feature set and rendering capabilities.

Key Features of Unreal Engine:

- **Photorealistic Rendering**: Unreal Engine excels in creating stunning visuals and realistic environments, thanks to its powerful rendering engine, dynamic lighting, and advanced particle systems.
- **Blueprint Visual Scripting**: Unreal's Blueprint system enables developers to create complex game logic using a visual interface, making it accessible for designers and artists.
- **C++ Programming**: For more advanced users, Unreal Engine provides extensive support for C++, allowing developers to write custom code and optimize performance.
- **Strong Multiplayer Support**: Unreal Engine is designed with multiplayer games in mind, offering features such as networking, replication, and dedicated server support.

3. Three.js

Three.js is a JavaScript library that simplifies the creation of 3D graphics for the web. It is not a full-fledged game engine like Unity or Unreal but is widely used for creating interactive 3D applications and visualizations in web browsers.

Key Features of Three.js:

- **Web-Based**: Three.js allows developers to create 3D content that runs directly in web browsers, making it an excellent choice for web developers and projects that require online accessibility.
- **Lightweight**: Being a library rather than a full engine, Three.js is lightweight and can be integrated into existing web applications easily.
- **Rich API**: Three.js provides a comprehensive API that supports various features, including geometry creation, material management, lighting, and camera control.
- **Compatibility**: Three.js works well with WebGL, enabling developers to leverage the GPU for rendering and achieving high-performance graphics in the browser.

Summary

When considering a 3D engine for game development, it is essential to evaluate the specific needs of your project and your expertise. Unity and Unreal Engine are powerful tools for creating high-quality games across various platforms, while Three.js is an excellent choice for web-based 3D applications. Understanding the strengths and weaknesses of each engine will help you make informed decisions in your game development journey.

Picking the Right Engine for Beginners

Choosing the right 3D engine as a beginner can significantly impact your learning experience and development process. Here are some factors to consider when selecting an engine:

1. Project Type

Different engines cater to different types of projects. If you are interested in developing traditional games, Unity or Unreal Engine would be more suitable. If your focus is on web-based applications or interactive visualizations, Three.js would be the ideal choice.

2. Ease of Use

For beginners, the learning curve is a critical factor. Unity is often praised for its intuitive interface and comprehensive tutorials, making it accessible for newcomers. Unreal Engine, while powerful, can be more complex due to its advanced features, which may be overwhelming for those just starting. Three.js has a simpler API but requires familiarity with JavaScript and web development concepts.

3. Community and Resources

The availability of community support and resources can greatly enhance your learning experience. Unity has a large and active community, with numerous forums, tutorials, and documentation available. Unreal Engine also has robust resources, but they may be more focused on advanced topics. Three.js, being a web library, has a smaller community compared to the other two but offers valuable documentation and examples.

4. Asset Availability

Consider the availability of assets and plugins that can speed up your development process. Unity's Asset Store provides a vast library of assets, scripts, and tools. Unreal Engine has its Marketplace, while Three.js users may find resources in the wider JavaScript and web development community.

5. *Future Goals*

Consider your long-term goals in game development. If you aim to work in the gaming industry or develop large-scale projects, starting with Unreal Engine may be beneficial. However, if you plan to create smaller games or interactive applications, Unity or Three.js might be a better fit.

Summary

Ultimately, the best engine for beginners depends on individual preferences and project goals. Unity is often recommended for its ease of use and versatility, while Unreal Engine is suited for those seeking to create high-fidelity graphics. Three.js is ideal for web developers looking to explore 3D graphics in the browser. The key is to experiment with different engines and find the one that aligns with your interests and aspirations.

Setting Up Your Development Environment

Once you have selected a 3D engine, the next step is to set up your development environment. This process involves installing the necessary software, configuring settings, and preparing your workspace for development. Below are the steps to set up your development environment for Unity and Three.js.

Setting Up Unity

1. **Download and Install Unity Hub**

- Visit the Unity website and download Unity Hub, the application that manages Unity installations and projects.
- Follow the installation instructions for your operating system.

1. **Install Unity Editor**

- Open Unity Hub and navigate to the "Installs" tab.
- Click on "Add" to install a new version of Unity. Choose the latest stable release and any additional components you may need (e.g., support for specific platforms like Android or iOS).

1. **Create a New Project**

- Once Unity is installed, go to the "Projects" tab in Unity Hub and click on "New Project."
- Choose a template (e.g., 3D, 2D) based on your project type and set the project name and location. Click "Create" to launch the Unity Editor.

1. **Familiarize Yourself with the Interface**

- Spend some time exploring the Unity Editor interface, including the Scene view, Game view, Hierarchy, Inspector, and Project panels. Understanding the layout will help you navigate the development process more efficiently.

1. **Install Additional Packages**

- Unity's Package Manager allows you to add various tools and features to your project. Access the Package Manager via the "Window" menu and search for packages like Post Processing or TextMeshPro to enhance your project.

Setting Up Three.js

1. **Download or Include Three.js**

- You can either download the Three.js library from the official website or include it directly in your HTML file using a CDN link. To use a CDN, simply add the following script tag in the head of your HTML file:

```
html
Copy code
<script
src="https://cdnjs.cloudflare.com/ajax/libs/three.js/r128/three.min.
js"></script>
```

1. Set Up a Basic HTML Structure

- Create an HTML file with a basic structure. Include a canvas element where the 3D scene will be rendered:

```
html
Copy code
<!DOCTYPE html>
<html lang="en">
<head>
    <meta charset="UTF-8">
    <meta name="viewport" content="width=device-width,
    initial-scale=1.0">
    <title>Three.js Example</title>
    <script
    src="https://cdnjs.cloudflare.com/ajax/libs/three.js/r128/three
    .min.js"></script> </head>
<body>
    <canvas id="myCanvas"></canvas>
    <script src="app.js"></script>
</body>
</html>
```

1. Create a JavaScript File

- Create a JavaScript file (e.g., app.js) where you will write the code to initialize the Three.js scene, camera, and renderer.

1. **Set Up Your First Three.js Scene**

- In your app.js file, write the basic code to create a Three.js scene:

```javascript
Copy code
// Set up scene, camera, and renderer
const scene = new THREE.Scene();
const camera = new THREE.PerspectiveCamera(75, window.innerWidth
/ window.innerHeight, 0.1, 1000);
const renderer = new THREE.WebGLRenderer({ canvas:
document.getElementById('myCanvas') });

renderer.setSize(window.innerWidth, window.innerHeight);
document.body.appendChild(renderer.domElement);

// Create a simple cube
const geometry = new THREE.BoxGeometry();
const material = new THREE.MeshBasicMaterial({ color: 0x00ff00 });
const cube = new THREE.Mesh(geometry, material);
scene.add(cube);

camera.position.z = 5;

// Animation loop
function animate() {
    requestAnimationFrame(animate);
    cube.rotation.x += 0.01;
    cube.rotation.y += 0.01;
    renderer.render(scene, camera);
}
animate();
```

Summary

Setting up your development environment is a crucial step in the game development process. Whether you choose Unity or Three.js, following the installation and configuration steps will prepare you to start creating your 3D projects. Familiarizing yourself with the interface and capabilities of the chosen engine will streamline your development journey.

First Look at a 3D Engine (Unity or Three.js Example)

Example: Creating a Simple 3D Scene in Unity

Now that you have set up Unity, let's create a simple 3D scene to familiarize ourselves with the engine's features and workflow.

1. **Open Your Unity Project**

- Launch Unity Hub, select your project, and open it.

1. **Create a New Scene**

- In the Unity Editor, go to "File" > "New Scene" to create a new scene. You can choose to save the default scene or create a new one.

1. **Add a Ground Plane**

- Right-click in the Hierarchy panel and select "3D Object" > "Plane." This will create a ground surface for your scene.

1. **Add a Cube**

- Right-click in the Hierarchy again and select "3D Object" > "Cube." This will add a cube to your scene.

1. **Adjust the Cube's Position**

- With the cube selected, go to the Inspector panel and adjust its Transform component. Set the position to (0, 0.5, 0) to raise the cube above the ground plane.

1. **Add a Light Source**

- To illuminate your scene, right-click in the Hierarchy and select "Light" > "Directional Light." This will add a light source to your scene, casting shadows and enhancing the overall look.

1. **Create a Camera**

- Unity automatically adds a Main Camera to your scene, but you can adjust its position to get a better view. Select the Main Camera and change its Transform position to (0, 1, -5) to move it back and up.

1. **Play the Scene**

- Click the "Play" button at the top of the Unity Editor to enter Play Mode. You can rotate the scene view and see your cube illuminated on the ground.

1. **Adding Interactivity (Optional)**

- To add some interactivity, you can create a simple script to rotate the cube. In the Project panel, right-click in the Assets folder, select "Create" > "C# Script," and name it RotateCube.
- Open the script and add the following code:

```csharp
Copy code
using UnityEngine;

public class RotateCube : MonoBehaviour
{
    void Update()
    {
        transform.Rotate(new Vector3(15, 30, 45) *
        Time.deltaTime);
    }
}
```

- Save the script and drag it onto the cube in the Hierarchy panel. Now, when you play the scene, the cube will rotate continuously.

Example: Creating a Simple 3D Scene in Three.js

Now let's create a similar simple 3D scene using Three.js to get a hands-on understanding of how it works.

1. **Set Up Your Project**

- Follow the previous steps to create an HTML file and a JavaScript file for your Three.js project.

1. **Add the Three.js Script**

- Include the Three.js library in your HTML file using a CDN link as shown earlier.

1. **Create the Basic Scene**

- In your app.js file, start by setting up the scene, camera, and renderer:

```javascript
Copy code
const scene = new THREE.Scene();
const camera = new THREE.PerspectiveCamera(75, window.innerWidth
/ window.innerHeight, 0.1, 1000);
const renderer = new THREE.WebGLRenderer({ canvas:
document.getElementById('myCanvas') });

renderer.setSize(window.innerWidth, window.innerHeight);
document.body.appendChild(renderer.domElement);
```

1. **Add a Ground Plane**

- Create a plane to act as the ground:

```javascript
Copy code
const planeGeometry = new THREE.PlaneGeometry(5, 5);
const planeMaterial = new THREE.MeshBasicMaterial({ color:
0x00ff00, side: THREE.DoubleSide });
const plane = new THREE.Mesh(planeGeometry, planeMaterial);
plane.rotation.x = Math.PI / 2; // Rotate the plane to be
horizontal
scene.add(plane);
```

1. **Add a Cube**

- Create a cube to place on the ground:

```javascript
Copy code
const cubeGeometry = new THREE.BoxGeometry();
const cubeMaterial = new THREE.MeshBasicMaterial({ color:
0x0000ff });
const cube = new THREE.Mesh(cubeGeometry, cubeMaterial);
cube.position.y = 0.5; // Raise the cube above the ground
scene.add(cube);
```

1. **Position the Camera**

- Set the camera's position to get a good view of the scene:

```javascript
Copy code
camera.position.z = 5;
```

1. **Animation Loop**

- Set up an animation loop to rotate the cube:

```javascript
Copy code
function animate() {
    requestAnimationFrame(animate);
    cube.rotation.x += 0.01;
    cube.rotation.y += 0.01;
    renderer.render(scene, camera);
}
animate();
```

1. **Run the Project**

- Open the HTML file in a web browser to see your 3D scene. You should see a rotating cube on a green plane.

We have just explored popular 3D engines like Unity, Unreal Engine, and Three.js. Understanding the strengths and weaknesses of each engine is crucial for making informed decisions in your development journey. We also discussed how to pick the right engine for beginners based on project type, ease of use, community support, asset availability, and future goals. Finally, we covered the steps for setting up your development environment and provided examples of creating simple 3D scenes in both Unity and Three.js. With this foundation, you are now prepared to delve deeper into the world of 3D game development and unleash your creativity.

Chapter 4: 3D Game Objects and Modeling

Introduction to 3D Models

3D models are the building blocks of any three-dimensional environment in games. These models represent objects, characters, and environments within a 3D space, defined by their geometric properties. A 3D model consists of vertices, edges, and faces that create a mesh, which can be manipulated to create intricate designs and visual effects.

1. What is a 3D Model?

A 3D model is a mathematical representation of a three-dimensional object. It exists in a three-dimensional space, defined by a coordinate system (usually the Cartesian coordinate system). Each model is composed of:

- **Vertices**: The fundamental points in 3D space, defined by their coordinates (x, y, z). Each vertex is a corner or a point where edges meet.
- **Edges**: The lines connecting two vertices, forming the outline of the model. Edges give shape to the model and define its structure.
- **Faces**: The flat surfaces enclosed by edges. Faces are typically made up of triangles (triangular meshes) or quadrilaterals (quads), which collectively

define the visual appearance of the model.

2. Types of 3D Models

3D models can be categorized into various types, depending on their complexity and intended use:

- **Static Models**: These models do not change or animate during gameplay. Examples include environmental objects like trees, rocks, and buildings.
- **Animated Models**: These models can change shape or position, typically used for characters and creatures that require movement and articulation.
- **Procedural Models**: Created algorithmically rather than manually designed, these models can dynamically change based on parameters. Procedural generation is often used for landscapes and large-scale environments.

3. Applications of 3D Models

3D models play a critical role in a wide range of applications beyond gaming, including:

- **Film and Animation**: Used for visual effects, character animation, and set design.
- **Architecture**: Architectural visualization uses 3D models to create realistic representations of buildings and environments before construction.
- **Virtual Reality (VR) and Augmented Reality (AR)**: 3D models are essential for creating immersive experiences in VR and AR applications.
- **Medical Visualization**: Used for simulating anatomical structures and medical procedures.

Understanding the fundamental aspects of 3D models is crucial for game developers, as these models form the visual core of any game environment.

Mastering the creation and manipulation of 3D models opens up a world of possibilities for building engaging and immersive experiences.

Working with 3D Models in Your Game Engine

Once you have created or acquired 3D models, the next step is to integrate them into your game engine. This process involves importing, manipulating, and optimizing models for use in your game. Different engines have unique workflows, but the general principles remain similar across platforms.

1. Importing 3D Models

Most modern game engines support a variety of file formats for importing 3D models. Common formats include:

- **FBX (Filmbox)**: A widely used format that supports complex animations, textures, and rigging. FBX is compatible with many 3D modeling applications, making it a popular choice for game developers.
- **OBJ (Wavefront Object)**: A simpler format that primarily supports geometry (vertices, edges, and faces) without animation data. OBJ files are often used for static models and are easily imported into most game engines.
- **GLTF (GL Transmission Format)**: An open-standard format designed for transmitting 3D models over the web. It supports animations, materials, and textures, making it suitable for real-time applications.

To import models into your game engine, you typically follow these steps:

1. **Export the Model from Your 3D Modeling Software**: Use software like Blender, Maya, or 3ds Max to create your model and export it in the desired format (FBX, OBJ, GLTF, etc.).
2. **Import the Model into the Game Engine**: Open your game engine (e.g., Unity, Unreal Engine) and use the import functionality to bring in

46

your model. This process may involve dragging the file into the project window or using a menu option to import assets.

3. **Adjust Import Settings**: After importing, you may need to adjust the import settings to ensure the model is properly scaled, oriented, and configured for use in the game.

2. Manipulating 3D Models

Once your 3D model is imported into the game engine, you can manipulate it within the scene. Key operations include:

- **Transformations**: Adjusting the position, rotation, and scale of the model using the Transform tool. These transformations are typically done through the Inspector panel in Unity or the Details panel in Unreal Engine.
- **Materials and Textures**: Applying materials and textures to the model enhances its visual appearance. Most engines allow you to create or import materials that define the surface properties, including color, texture, and reflectivity.
- **Colliders**: Adding colliders to models enables physical interactions with other objects in the game. Colliders define the shape of the object for physics calculations, allowing for accurate collision detection and response.
- **Animation**: If your model is animated, you can set up animations within the engine. This may involve creating an Animator Controller in Unity or using the Animation Blueprint in Unreal Engine.

3. Optimizing 3D Models

To ensure optimal performance in your game, it is essential to optimize your 3D models. Large and complex models can lead to performance issues, especially in real-time applications. Key optimization techniques include:

- **Reduce Polygon Count**: Simplifying the mesh can reduce the number of polygons, improving rendering performance without sacrificing visual quality. Use tools like the Decimate modifier in Blender to lower the polygon count.
- **Level of Detail (LOD)**: Implementing LOD techniques allows you to use simpler models for objects that are farther away from the camera. This reduces the rendering workload while maintaining visual fidelity for closer objects.
- **Texture Optimization**: Use texture atlases to combine multiple textures into a single image, reducing the number of texture loads during rendering. Also, consider using lower-resolution textures for distant objects.
- **Bake Lighting**: For static objects, baking lighting information into textures can reduce the need for real-time calculations, improving performance.

By mastering the process of working with 3D models in your game engine, you will be well-equipped to create engaging and visually appealing experiences for players.

Primitive Shapes: Cubes, Spheres, Cylinders

In 3D modeling, primitive shapes serve as the foundational building blocks for more complex structures. Understanding how to work with these shapes is crucial for creating 3D objects quickly and efficiently.

1. Cubes

Cubes are one of the simplest and most versatile primitive shapes in 3D modeling. They consist of six square faces, twelve edges, and eight vertices. Cubes are often used for:

- **Basic Structure**: As a starting point for more complex models, cubes can be manipulated (scaled, extruded, or subdivided) to create various shapes and forms.

- **Game Objects**: Cubes can represent buildings, platforms, and other solid objects in a game environment.
- **Collision Detection**: Cubes are commonly used for creating colliders due to their straightforward geometry, making it easy to calculate collisions in a game.

Creating and Manipulating Cubes

In most 3D modeling software and game engines, creating a cube is straightforward. Here's how to do it:

- **In Unity**: Right-click in the Hierarchy panel, select "3D Object," and then choose "Cube." The cube will appear in the Scene view, and you can use the Transform tool to adjust its position, rotation, and scale.
- **In Blender**: Press Shift + A to open the Add menu, then select "Mesh" > "Cube." You can enter Edit mode (Tab key) to manipulate the vertices, edges, and faces of the cube.

2. Spheres

Spheres are another fundamental primitive shape, defined by a continuous surface with no edges or vertices. They are used to represent:

- **Round Objects**: Spheres can simulate various round objects, such as balls, planets, and characters' heads.
- **Collision Shapes**: Spherical colliders are often used for dynamic objects that require smooth interactions, as they simplify collision detection.

Creating and Manipulating Spheres

Creating and manipulating spheres is similar to creating cubes:

- **In Unity**: Right-click in the Hierarchy panel, select "3D Object," and then choose "Sphere." You can adjust its size and position in the Scene view.

- **In Blender**: Press Shift + A, select "Mesh," and then choose "UV Sphere" or "Icosphere" for different spherical geometries. You can modify the sphere's topology in Edit mode.

3. Cylinders

Cylinders are elongated shapes defined by a circular base and a specified height. They are commonly used for:

- **Pillars and Columns**: Cylinders can represent structural elements in a scene, such as pillars in a building.
- **Wheels and Barrels**: Cylinders are ideal for modeling round objects that require a continuous surface.

Creating and Manipulating Cylinders

Creating and manipulating cylinders follows the same process as cubes and spheres:

- **In Unity**: Right-click in the Hierarchy panel, select "3D Object," and then choose "Cylinder." You can modify its height and radius in the Inspector.

In Blender: Press Shift + A, select "Mesh," and then choose "Cylinder." You can enter Edit mode to edit its vertices, edges, and faces to achieve the desired shape.

- 4. Combining Primitive Shapes

Primitive shapes can be combined to create more complex models. This technique is widely used in both modeling and game development, as it allows developers to quickly build intricate structures without the need for detailed modeling from scratch.

- **Union Operations**: In many 3D modeling tools, you can perform union operations to combine two or more primitive shapes into a single mesh. This is often called "Boolean operations." For example, you could take two cylinders and join them to create a pillar with a rounded top.
- **Subtraction Operations**: Similarly, subtraction allows you to remove portions of a primitive shape. This is useful for creating holes or indentations in models.
- **Extruding Shapes**: Extruding allows you to extend faces of primitive shapes, creating new geometry. For example, selecting the top face of a cube and extruding it upward can create a tower.

By utilizing primitive shapes effectively, you can streamline your modeling process, saving time and effort while achieving complex designs.

- Importing Assets: FBX, OBJ, and More

Once you have created your 3D models, the next step is to import them into your game engine for use in your project. Different file formats are available for importing assets, each with its advantages and limitations. Understanding how to use these formats is crucial for effective asset management in your game development workflow.

- 1. FBX (Filmbox)

FBX is one of the most popular file formats for 3D models and animations. Originally developed by Kaydara and later acquired by Autodesk, FBX supports a wide range of features that make it ideal for game development.

- **Key Features of FBX:**
- **Animation Support**: FBX files can store complex animations, including skeletal animations and morph targets, making it a versatile choice for

animated characters and objects.

- **Material and Texture Information**: FBX supports the inclusion of material and texture information, allowing you to maintain the visual fidelity of your models when importing them into a game engine.
- **Rigging Information**: FBX can contain rigging data, enabling you to import fully rigged characters ready for animation in the game engine.

Importing FBX Files

To import an FBX file into a game engine:

- **In Unity**: Drag the FBX file into the Project panel. Unity will automatically generate a prefab of the model, including any associated animations and materials. You can then drag the prefab into your scene.
- **In Unreal Engine**: Use the "Import" option in the Content Browser to bring in your FBX file. Unreal Engine will allow you to configure import settings, such as animation, material assignment, and scale.
- 2. OBJ (Wavefront Object)

OBJ is a simple and widely supported file format for 3D models. It primarily contains geometry data, making it suitable for static models without animations.

- **Key Features of OBJ**:
- **Simple Geometry**: OBJ files store vertex positions, texture coordinates, normals, and face definitions, making them easy to read and manipulate.
- **Material Support**: OBJ files can be accompanied by MTL files, which define materials for the model, including texture references and properties.

Importing OBJ Files

To import an OBJ file into a game engine:

- **In Unity**: Just like FBX, you can drag the OBJ file into the Project panel.

Unity will create a mesh from the file. If the OBJ has a corresponding MTL file, Unity will also apply the materials automatically.

- **In Unreal Engine**: Similar to FBX, you can import OBJ files using the "Import" option in the Content Browser. Unreal Engine will create a static mesh asset from the OBJ file.
- 3. GLTF (GL Transmission Format)

GLTF is an open-standard file format designed for efficient transmission and loading of 3D models in real-time applications, particularly on the web.

- **Key Features of GLTF:**
- **Compact Size**: GLTF is optimized for size, making it suitable for web applications where loading times are critical.
- **PBR Support**: GLTF supports physically-based rendering (PBR), allowing for realistic materials and lighting effects.
- **Animation and Scene Graphs**: GLTF can store animations and scene hierarchy information, enabling complex 3D scenes to be represented.

Importing GLTF Files

To import GLTF files into a game engine:

- **In Unity**: Unity has a GLTF utility available through the Asset Store or as part of the newer versions, allowing you to import GLTF files directly.
- **In Unreal Engine**: You can also import GLTF files using third-party plugins or by converting them to FBX for more straightforward import.
- 4. Other Formats

In addition to FBX, OBJ, and GLTF, there are other file formats used for 3D models:

- **3DS**: An older format that supports geometry and materials but is less commonly used in modern game development due to its limitations.
- **DAE (Collada)**: An interchange file format that supports multiple types

of data, including physics, animations, and scene hierarchy. While not as popular as FBX, it can still be useful for specific applications.

- **PLY (Polygon File Format)**: Often used for 3D scanning and printing, PLY files can contain geometry and color information. They are less commonly used in game development.

In this chapter, we explored the fundamentals of 3D game objects and modeling. Understanding 3D models, their components, and how to manipulate them is essential for creating engaging game environments. We discussed the role of primitive shapes—cubes, spheres, and cylinders—as foundational building blocks for more complex designs. Furthermore, we examined various file formats for importing assets, including FBX, OBJ, and GLTF, and how to effectively use these formats in your game engine.

- By mastering the process of working with 3D models and importing assets, you will be well-equipped to develop rich, immersive gaming experiences that captivate players. As you progress in your game development journey, continue to experiment with different modeling techniques and asset formats to enhance your skills and creativity in creating stunning 3D worlds.

Chapter 5: Lighting and Shading in 3D

ighting and shading are pivotal elements in 3D game development that significantly influence the aesthetics, mood, and realism of a game. They help create immersive environments and guide players' emotions and actions within the game world. In this chapter, we will explore how lighting impacts game aesthetics, examine different types of lighting, discuss shadows and reflections, and delve into the world of shaders to understand surface effects.

How Lighting Impacts Game Aesthetics

Lighting plays a crucial role in setting the tone and atmosphere of a game. It can evoke emotions, direct attention, and enhance the overall storytelling experience. Here's how lighting impacts game aesthetics:

1. Mood and Atmosphere

Different lighting setups can convey various moods and atmospheres. For example:

- **Bright, Warm Lighting**: Often associated with happiness and positivity, bright lighting with warm tones can create an inviting and cheerful environment. This lighting is frequently used in family-friendly games or those set in vibrant settings.
- **Dim, Cool Lighting**: Low-light settings with cooler tones can evoke

feelings of tension or fear. Horror games often use such lighting to create suspense and unease, immersing players in a world filled with uncertainty.

- **Dynamic Lighting**: Using changing lighting conditions—such as day-night cycles—can significantly impact gameplay and storytelling. Transitioning from bright daylight to eerie twilight can alter the player's experience, prompting them to adapt their strategies.

2. Visual Hierarchy

Lighting can direct players' attention to specific areas or objects within a scene. By highlighting certain elements with brighter light or contrasting colors, developers can guide players through their environments. This technique is often used in puzzle-solving scenarios or key narrative moments to emphasize important items or pathways.

3. Realism and Immersion

Realistic lighting contributes to the believability of a game world. Accurate representation of how light interacts with objects enhances immersion and draws players into the experience. Techniques like global illumination simulate how light bounces off surfaces and interacts with the environment, creating a more lifelike appearance.

4. Color and Texture Enhancement

Lighting can enhance the perceived color and texture of materials in a game. Properly positioned light sources can bring out the richness of textures, making surfaces appear more detailed and engaging. For instance, a rough stone wall can look more rugged and textured under the right lighting conditions, adding depth to the visual experience.

5. Storytelling and Narrative

Lighting can be a powerful narrative tool. Changes in lighting can signify important plot points or character emotions. For example, a sudden shift to dark lighting might indicate danger or a dramatic turn in the story, while a warm glow might signal a safe haven or a moment of reflection.

Understanding how lighting impacts game aesthetics allows developers to create visually compelling and emotionally resonant experiences. Mastery of lighting techniques is essential for achieving the desired atmosphere and enhancing the overall quality of a game.

Types of Lighting: Point, Directional, Spot

Different types of lighting serve various purposes in 3D environments. Each type has distinct characteristics and uses, allowing developers to create dynamic and engaging scenes. Below, we explore the three main types of lighting commonly used in 3D game development: point, directional, and spot lighting.

1. Point Lighting

Point lights are omnidirectional light sources that emit light uniformly in all directions from a single point in space. They are similar to light bulbs or candles, casting light on surrounding objects and creating a soft, diffuse illumination.

Characteristics of Point Lights:

- **Distance Attenuation**: The intensity of light diminishes with distance. The further an object is from the light source, the less illuminated it becomes. This effect can be controlled using attenuation settings, allowing developers to customize how light behaves in their scenes.
- **Soft Shadows**: Point lights typically produce soft, diffused shadows due to their spherical nature. The edges of the shadows are less defined,

creating a more natural look in environments.

Use Cases for Point Lights:

- **Ambient Lighting**: Point lights are often used to simulate ambient lighting in a room, providing a base level of illumination while still allowing for shadows and highlights.
- **Decorative Elements**: Point lights can be used as decorative lighting in specific areas, such as street lamps or chandeliers, enhancing the visual appeal of the environment.
- **Dynamic Lighting**: In some games, point lights can be animated or changed in intensity to create dynamic lighting effects that respond to gameplay, such as flickering torches in a dungeon.

2. Directional Lighting

Directional lights simulate sunlight or other distant light sources that produce parallel rays of light. Unlike point lights, directional lights do not have a defined position; instead, they illuminate the scene based on their direction.

Characteristics of Directional Lights:

- **Parallel Rays**: Light rays emitted from a directional light are parallel, resulting in consistent lighting across large distances. This creates sharp, defined shadows and a more uniform illumination.
- **No Distance Attenuation**: Directional lights do not diminish in intensity based on distance. Objects remain illuminated regardless of their distance from the light source.

Use Cases for Directional Lights:

- **Natural Light Simulation**: Directional lights are commonly used to simulate sunlight in outdoor environments. By positioning the light at an angle, developers can create realistic sun positions and corresponding shadows.

- **Flat Lighting Effects**: In some cases, directional lights can be used to create flat lighting effects, where objects are evenly lit without strong shadows. This technique can be useful for specific art styles or gameplay mechanics.
- **Realistic Shadows**: The sharp shadows produced by directional lights can add depth and realism to environments, making objects appear more grounded in the scene.

3. Spot Lighting

Spotlights are focused light sources that emit light in a specific cone shape. They are used to create targeted illumination and dramatic effects in 3D environments.

Characteristics of Spotlights:

- **Cone Shape**: Spotlights emit light in a cone shape, allowing developers to control the direction and spread of the light. This makes them ideal for highlighting specific areas or objects.
- **Falloff Settings**: Developers can adjust the intensity and angle of the spotlight to create soft or hard edges. This allows for greater control over the lighting effect and the atmosphere of the scene.

Use Cases for Spotlights:

- **Theatrical Effects**: Spotlights are often used in theatrical settings within games, such as illuminating characters or important objects during cutscenes or gameplay moments.
- **Environmental Highlighting**: Spotlights can be used to draw attention to specific areas or features in a game world, such as treasure chests or key objectives.
- **Dynamic Lighting**: Spotlights can be animated to follow characters

or events, creating a dynamic lighting experience that enhances the gameplay and narrative.

Summary of Lighting Types

Each type of lighting—point, directional, and spot—serves a specific purpose in 3D environments. Understanding the characteristics and applications of these lighting types allows developers to create visually stunning and immersive experiences that enhance gameplay and storytelling.

Shadows and Reflections

Shadows and reflections are critical components of 3D rendering that add depth and realism to game environments. They enhance the visual quality of a scene and provide players with valuable cues about the spatial relationships between objects.

1. Shadows

Shadows are the areas of darkness created when an object blocks light from reaching a surface. They play a vital role in establishing the three-dimensionality of a scene, providing depth and grounding objects within the environment.

Types of Shadows

- **Hard Shadows**: Produced by direct light sources, hard shadows have crisp, well-defined edges. They create strong contrasts and are typically associated with harsh lighting conditions.
- **Soft Shadows**: Soft shadows have blurred edges and create a more natural look. They occur when light is diffused or when multiple light sources contribute to the shadow. Soft shadows are commonly used to simulate natural lighting conditions.

Shadow Mapping Techniques

Different techniques are used to calculate and render shadows in real-time:

- **Shadow Mapping**: This technique involves rendering the scene from the perspective of the light source to create a shadow map. The map stores depth information for objects, allowing the engine to determine whether a pixel is in shadow when rendering the final image.
- **Ray Traced Shadows**: Ray tracing is a more advanced technique that simulates the way light interacts with surfaces to create accurate shadows. This method produces highly realistic shadows but requires more computational power.

Importance of Shadows

- **Depth Perception**: Shadows enhance depth perception by providing visual cues about the positioning and height of objects in a scene.
- **Realism**: Properly implemented shadows contribute to the overall realism of a game, making environments feel more believable and engaging.
- **Visual Interest**: Shadows add complexity to scenes, creating a visually appealing experience. They can enhance the aesthetic quality of a game, drawing players into the environment.

2. Reflections

Reflections occur when light bounces off surfaces, creating mirrored images of objects in a scene. Like shadows, reflections add realism and depth to 3D environments.

Types of Reflections

- **Specular Reflections**: These reflections occur on shiny surfaces, where light is reflected in a concentrated manner, creating highlights. Specular reflections are commonly seen on metallic or glossy surfaces.

- **Environment Reflections**: Environment reflections simulate how a surface reflects its surroundings. This technique is often used for water surfaces, glass, and other reflective materials.

Reflection Techniques

There are various methods for rendering reflections in 3D environments:

- **Cube Mapping**: This technique uses a cube map texture to simulate reflections. A cube map consists of six square textures that represent the view from the center of an object in all directions. Cube mapping is commonly used for reflective surfaces like water or polished metal.
- **Screen Space Reflections (SSR)**: SSR uses the information available on the screen to create reflections based on the scene's geometry and textures. This method is more efficient for real-time applications, but it has limitations, such as not capturing objects outside the screen view.
- **Ray Tracing**: Like shadows, ray tracing can be used to create highly accurate reflections. Ray tracing calculates how light rays interact with surfaces, producing realistic reflections that consider the scene's geometry and lighting conditions.

Importance of Reflections

- **Realism**: Accurate reflections enhance the realism of a scene, making objects appear more lifelike and grounded in their environment.
- **Visual Depth**: Reflections create a sense of depth and complexity within a scene, drawing players' attention and encouraging exploration.
- **Aesthetic Appeal**: Well-implemented reflections can elevate the visual quality of a game, adding polish and sophistication to the overall presentation.

Shaders: Understanding Surface Effects

Shaders are essential components in 3D graphics that define how surfaces interact with light and render visual effects. They are small programs that run on the GPU (Graphics Processing Unit) and control the rendering process, determining the appearance of materials and objects in a game.

1. What are Shaders?

Shaders are written in specialized programming languages such as GLSL (OpenGL Shading Language), HLSL (High-Level Shading Language), or Cg (C for Graphics). They define how vertices and pixels are processed, allowing developers to create a wide range of visual effects.

There are several types of shaders, each serving a specific purpose in the rendering pipeline:

- **Vertex Shaders**: Process vertex data, transforming 3D coordinates into screen space. Vertex shaders are responsible for applying transformations, lighting calculations, and passing data to fragment shaders.
- **Fragment Shaders (Pixel Shaders)**: Process pixel data and determine the final color and appearance of each pixel on the screen. Fragment shaders can apply textures, lighting effects, and other visual enhancements.
- **Geometry Shaders**: Optional shaders that operate on the geometry level, allowing for the creation or modification of geometric shapes in real-time. Geometry shaders are often used for effects like tessellation or particle generation.

2. Surface Shaders

Surface shaders are a specific type of shader used to define the visual properties of surfaces in 3D models. They simulate how light interacts with materials, including effects such as color, texture, reflectivity, and transparency.

Key Surface Effects

- **Diffuse Reflection**: The basic shading model that simulates how light scatters when it hits a rough surface. The Lambertian reflection model is commonly used for diffuse shading, where the brightness of a surface is determined by its angle to the light source.
- **Specular Reflection**: Simulates the shiny highlights on surfaces, providing a sense of glossiness and material quality. The Phong or Blinn-Phong reflection models are often used for calculating specular highlights.
- **Bump Mapping**: A technique used to simulate small surface details without increasing polygon count. Bump mapping uses a grayscale texture to alter the surface normals, creating the illusion of depth and texture.
- **Normal Mapping**: Similar to bump mapping, normal mapping uses a texture that stores normal information to create detailed surface effects. It allows for more complex lighting interactions and detailed surface appearances.
- **Transparency and Refraction**: Shaders can simulate transparent materials, allowing light to pass through while altering its path. Refraction shaders can create realistic effects for materials like glass or water.

3. Creating Custom Shaders

Developers can create custom shaders to achieve specific visual effects tailored to their game's aesthetics. Custom shaders offer flexibility and creativity, allowing artists to experiment with unique looks and interactions.

Shader Development Process

1. **Define the Effect**: Determine the visual effect you want to achieve (e.g., a glowing object, a reflective surface, or a stylized look).
2. **Write the Shader Code**: Use a shader programming language to write

the shader code, defining how vertices and pixels should be processed.

3. **Test and Iterate**: Integrate the shader into your game engine and test it in various lighting conditions. Adjust the code as needed to refine the effect and ensure it meets your vision.

4. **Optimize Performance**: Ensure that your custom shaders are efficient and do not negatively impact performance. Consider reducing calculations where possible and using simpler models where appropriate.

In this chapter, we explored the crucial role of lighting and shading in 3D game development. Lighting impacts game aesthetics by setting mood, enhancing realism, and guiding player attention. We discussed the three primary types of lighting—point, directional, and spot—each serving distinct purposes in creating dynamic environments.

We examined the importance of shadows and reflections in adding depth and realism to scenes, alongside the techniques used to render them effectively. Finally, we delved into shaders, understanding their role in defining surface effects and creating custom visual experiences.

By mastering lighting, shadows, reflections, and shaders, you can elevate your 3D game development skills, crafting immersive environments that engage and captivate players. As you continue your journey, experimenting with these elements will enhance the visual storytelling and artistic expression within your games.

Chapter 6: Textures and Materials

Textures and materials are essential components in 3D game development, providing the visual richness that brings models to life. They define the surface appearance of objects, influencing how light interacts with them and how players perceive the game world. In this chapter, we will explore the process of applying textures to 3D models, understanding UV mapping, creating realistic materials, and using normal maps and bump maps to enhance detail.

Applying Textures to 3D Models

Textures are 2D images that are wrapped around 3D models to give them color, detail, and realism. The process of applying textures involves several steps:

1. Choosing Textures

Selecting the right textures is crucial for achieving the desired look for your models. Textures can be sourced from various places:

- **Texture Libraries**: Many online libraries offer free or paid textures that can be downloaded and used in projects. Websites like **Textures.com**, **Poly Haven**, and **Quixel Megascans** provide high-quality textures for various materials.
- **Custom Textures**: Artists can create custom textures using image

editing software like Adobe Photoshop or GIMP. Custom textures allow for more control over the design and can be tailored to fit the specific aesthetic of a game.

2. Importing Textures

After selecting or creating textures, the next step is to import them into your game engine. Most engines support common image formats like PNG, JPEG, and TIFF. Here's how to import textures:

- **In Unity**: Drag and drop texture files into the Project panel. Unity automatically recognizes the imported textures, allowing you to create materials that use these textures.
- **In Unreal Engine**: Use the Content Browser to import texture files by clicking the "Import" button and selecting your image files. Unreal Engine will convert these files into texture assets.

3. Creating and Applying Materials

Once textures are imported, you need to create materials that utilize these textures. Materials define how the textures are applied to the surfaces of 3D models.

Creating Materials

- **In Unity**: Right-click in the Project panel, select "Create" > "Material." In the Inspector panel, you can assign the imported texture to the Albedo property. Adjust additional properties like smoothness and metallic settings to achieve the desired material effect.
- **In Unreal Engine**: Right-click in the Content Browser and choose "Material." Double-click the material to open the Material Editor, where you can drag and drop textures into the node graph. Connect the texture nodes to the appropriate inputs, such as Base Color, Roughness, and Specular.

Applying Materials to 3D Models

To apply the created materials to 3D models:

- **In Unity**: Select the 3D model in the Hierarchy and drag the material onto the model in the Scene view or assign it in the Inspector panel under the Mesh Renderer component.
- **In Unreal Engine**: Select the model in the viewport and assign the material in the Details panel under the Materials section.

4. Tile and Scale Textures

Often, textures need to be tiled or scaled to fit the models correctly. This is especially important for large surfaces where a single instance of a texture may not provide enough detail.

- **In Unity**: You can adjust the tiling settings in the material's Inspector panel. Modify the X and Y values in the Tiling section to control how the texture repeats across the model.
- **In Unreal Engine**: Use the Texture Coordinate node in the Material Editor to manipulate the UV scaling of the texture. Connect this node to the UV input of the texture sample node to adjust how the texture is mapped.

By applying textures effectively, you can enhance the visual fidelity of your 3D models, making them more engaging and believable within the game environment.

Understanding UV Mapping

UV mapping is a critical process in 3D modeling that involves projecting a 3D model's surface onto a 2D plane to apply textures accurately. It is essential for ensuring that textures fit properly on the model without distortion or seams.

1. What is UV Mapping?

UV mapping refers to the way a 2D texture is mapped onto a 3D object. The "U" and "V" denote the axes of the 2D texture, as "X," "Y," and "Z" are already used for the 3D coordinates.

UV Coordinates

- Each vertex of the 3D model is assigned a corresponding UV coordinate, which indicates where on the 2D texture the vertex will sample its color.
- The UV space typically ranges from (0, 0) at the bottom-left corner to (1, 1) at the top-right corner of the texture.

2. Creating UV Maps

Creating a UV map involves flattening the 3D model into a 2D representation. This process can be done in various 3D modeling software:

- **In Blender**: Enter Edit Mode, select the geometry, and use the UV Unwrap function (U key) to create the UV map. Blender offers several unwrapping methods, such as Smart UV Project and Cube Projection, depending on the model's shape.
- **In Maya**: Use the UV Editor to create and manipulate UV maps. Maya provides various tools for unwrapping, such as Automatic Mapping and Planar Mapping.

3. UV Mapping Techniques

Different techniques can be employed to achieve effective UV mapping:

- **Seams**: To minimize visible seams in the texture, carefully choose where to place UV seams on the model. Seams should ideally be placed in less noticeable areas or along edges where they can be hidden.
- **Laying Out UVs**: Arrange the UV islands (the flattened portions of the

model) efficiently within the UV space. Aim to maximize texture space usage while avoiding overlapping UVs unless specifically desired for shared texturing.

- **Scaling UVs**: Scale UV islands according to the level of detail needed. Larger UV islands will sample more texture detail, while smaller islands will sample less.

4. Testing UV Maps

After creating UV maps, it's essential to test them to ensure textures apply correctly:

- **Check for Distortion**: Apply a checkerboard texture to the model to visualize UV mapping. This will help identify areas where textures may be stretched or distorted.
- **Adjust UVs**: If any issues are identified, go back into the UV editing mode and make adjustments as necessary to improve the UV layout.

Understanding UV mapping is crucial for creating high-quality textures and ensuring that they fit accurately on 3D models. By mastering this technique, developers can create more detailed and visually appealing game assets.

Creating Realistic Materials (Metal, Wood, Glass, etc.)

Creating realistic materials involves understanding how different surfaces interact with light and how to replicate these interactions in a game engine. Each material type has unique properties that define its appearance and behavior.

1. Metal Materials

Metal materials are characterized by their reflectivity and specular highlights. They typically have low roughness and high metallic values.

Creating Metal Materials

- **Base Color**: Use a color that represents the metal (e.g., silver, gold, copper). The base color should not be too saturated, as metals often have subtle hues.
- **Metallic Property**: Set the metallic value to 1 (or 100%) in your material settings to achieve a fully metallic look. This instructs the engine to treat the surface as a metal.
- **Roughness**: Adjust the roughness value to control how shiny or dull the surface appears. A value close to 0 will create a highly reflective surface, while a higher value will produce a more diffused reflection.
- **Normal Map**: Consider using a normal map to add surface details, such as scratches or dents, which can enhance the realism of the metal material.

2. Wood Materials

Wood materials are defined by their texture, grain, and color. They can vary widely based on the type of wood being represented.

Creating Wood Materials

- **Base Color**: Use a color that reflects the wood type (e.g., light oak, dark walnut). The color can be slightly more saturated than metal materials.
- **Texture**: Apply a wood texture that represents the grain and patterns typical of wood. Textures can be sourced from texture libraries or created in image editing software.
- **Roughness**: Wood surfaces are generally more diffuse than metals. Set the roughness value to a moderate level (0.4 - 0.6) to simulate the natural look of wood.

- **Normal Map**: Use a normal map to add depth and detail to the wood grain, enhancing the visual interest of the material.

3. Glass Materials

Glass materials are characterized by their transparency, refraction, and reflections. Creating realistic glass requires a good understanding of how light interacts with transparent surfaces.

Creating Glass Materials

- **Base Color**: Glass is typically colorless, but tinted glass can have a subtle hue. Use a very light color with low saturation for clear glass.
- **Transparency**: Set the transparency value to allow light to pass through the material. In most engines, this can be achieved by adjusting the alpha value or transparency setting.
- **Roughness**: Glass is usually smooth, so set the roughness value close to 0 for clear glass. For frosted glass, increase the roughness value to simulate diffusion.
- **Refraction**: Set the index of refraction (IOR) to around 1.5 for glass, which simulates how light bends as it passes through the material.
- **Reflection**: Glass materials also reflect their environment. Use a reflection map or enable real-time reflections to create a realistic glass appearance.

4. Creating Other Materials

In addition to metal, wood, and glass, various other materials can be created using similar principles. Here are a few examples:

- **Plastic**: Use vibrant colors with moderate reflectivity. Set the roughness to a low value for shiny plastics, and consider using a normal map for added detail.
- **Fabric**: Textiles often have unique textures and patterns. Use a fabric

texture, set moderate roughness, and adjust the color to match the desired fabric type.

- **Stone**: For rocky surfaces, use a rough texture with subdued colors. Set the roughness to a higher value to create a rough appearance, and consider using displacement maps for additional detail.

Using Normal Maps and Bump Maps for Detail

Normal maps and bump maps are essential tools for adding detail and texture to 3D models without increasing the polygon count. They enhance surface details and improve realism by simulating complex features.

1. Bump Maps

Bump maps are grayscale textures that simulate surface detail by altering the surface normals of a model. They create the illusion of depth and texture without changing the actual geometry.

How Bump Maps Work

- **Grayscale Values**: The grayscale values in a bump map determine the height of the surface. White areas appear raised, while black areas are recessed.
- **Surface Normals**: Bump maps modify the normals of the surface, affecting how light interacts with it. This creates the illusion of depth and detail, making surfaces appear more complex.

Creating and Applying Bump Maps

- **Create a Bump Map**: Use image editing software to create a grayscale texture representing the desired surface detail. For example, create a bump map for a brick wall where the bricks are raised compared to the mortar.
- **Apply the Bump Map**: In your game engine, assign the bump map to

the appropriate input in the material settings. Adjust the bump strength to control the intensity of the effect.

2. Normal Maps

Normal maps are more advanced than bump maps, providing a greater level of detail and realism. They use RGB color values to represent surface normals, allowing for more complex lighting interactions.

How Normal Maps Work

- **RGB Representation**: Each pixel in a normal map represents a normal vector in 3D space. The red channel corresponds to the X-axis, the green channel to the Y-axis, and the blue channel to the Z-axis.
- **Detailed Surface Simulation**: Normal maps can simulate small details like scratches, wrinkles, and bumps, making surfaces appear more complex without adding geometry.

Creating and Applying Normal Maps

- **Create a Normal Map**: Use specialized tools like **xNormal**, **Crazy-Bump**, or built-in features in programs like Substance Painter to generate normal maps from high-resolution models or textures.
- **Apply the Normal Map**: In your game engine, assign the normal map to the normal input in the material settings. Ensure that the normal map is properly configured, so it interacts correctly with light.

3. Combining Normal Maps and Bump Maps

Both normal maps and bump maps can be used together to enhance surface details further. For instance, you might use a normal map for the overall surface detail and a bump map for specific features.

Summary

In this chapter, we explored the crucial role of textures and materials in 3D game development. We discussed the process of applying textures to models, understanding UV mapping, and creating realistic materials for various surface types. We also examined the use of normal maps and bump maps to enhance detail without increasing polygon counts.

By mastering the techniques of texturing and material creation, you can significantly improve the visual quality of your 3D models, creating engaging and immersive experiences for players. As you continue your journey in game development, experimenting with different textures and materials will enhance your artistic skills and help you craft more compelling game worlds.

Chapter 7: 3D Object Movement and Rotation

I ntroduction to 3D Object Movement and Rotation

Movement and rotation are fundamental to any 3D game environment. Players expect objects to move and interact naturally, whether it's a character running across a landscape, an enemy flying through the air, or a box being pushed by the player. To achieve these dynamic interactions, understanding how to manipulate objects in 3D space using transformations like position, rotation, and scale is essential. This chapter delves deep into the core principles of 3D object manipulation, how physics engines handle forces and collisions, and how to implement various movement patterns such as jumping, running, and flying. Additionally, we will explore camera control techniques for both first-person and third-person perspectives, enabling you to create immersive experiences for your players.

Transforming Objects: Position, Rotation, Scale

In 3D game development, every object has a "transform" component, which defines its position, rotation, and scale in 3D space. Mastering these transformations is key to animating objects, characters, and other game elements, allowing you to create smooth, dynamic, and believable motion in your game world.

Manipulating Position

The position of a 3D object refers to its location in the game world along the X, Y, and Z axes. The X-axis typically represents horizontal movement, the Y-axis represents vertical movement (such as jumping or flying), and the Z-axis often represents depth, moving objects closer or farther away from the camera.

Here's an example in Unity that demonstrates how to modify the position of an object using its transform component:

```csharp
Copy code
void Update() {
    transform.position += new Vector3(0, 0, speed *
    Time.deltaTime);
}
```

In this code, we move the object forward along the Z-axis, updating its position frame by frame based on the speed variable. The Time.deltaTime ensures that the movement is smooth and framerate-independent.

Rotating Objects

Rotation involves turning an object around one or more axes (X, Y, or Z). In 3D games, controlling rotation is vital for creating dynamic scenes, allowing players to aim, look around, or manipulate objects. Rotation can be handled using Euler angles (measured in degrees) or quaternions (used for smooth, interpolation-friendly rotations).

In Unity, rotating an object might look like this:

```csharp
Copy code
void Update() {
    transform.Rotate(new Vector3(0, rotationSpeed *
    Time.deltaTime, 0));
}
```

Here, the object rotates around the Y-axis at a speed defined by the rotationSpeed variable. Using Time.deltaTime ensures consistent rotation across different frame rates.

Scaling Objects

Scaling changes the size of an object, either uniformly (same size change on all axes) or non-uniformly (different size change on individual axes). Scaling is useful for enlarging or shrinking objects dynamically, such as making enemies grow larger as they get stronger or shrinking objects as they move away from the player.

Here's a simple example of scaling an object in Unity:

```csharp
Copy code
void Update() {
    if (Input.GetKey(KeyCode.Space)) {
        transform.localScale += new Vector3(0.1f, 0.1f, 0.1f);
    }
}
```

In this case, pressing the space bar increases the object's size by 0.1 units along all axes each frame.

Physics in 3D: Forces, Gravity, and Collisions

While directly manipulating position, rotation, and scale works for simple scenarios, more complex and realistic interactions in 3D games require physics. Physics engines handle object movement and interactions through forces, gravity, and collisions, creating lifelike behavior in the game world.

Applying Forces to Objects

A fundamental aspect of physics-based movement is the application of forces. Forces can be applied to objects to simulate real-world behavior, such as pushing, pulling, or throwing objects. Unity and Unreal Engine have built-in physics systems that allow developers to apply forces to objects using rigidbody components.

Here's an example of applying a force to an object in Unity:

```csharp
Copy code
void Update() {
    if (Input.GetKeyDown(KeyCode.Space)) {
        Rigidbody rb = GetComponent<Rigidbody>();
        rb.AddForce(Vector3.up * jumpForce, ForceMode.Impulse);
    }
}
```

In this example, pressing the space bar applies an upward force to the object, simulating a jump. The ForceMode.Impulse makes the force instantaneous, giving the object an immediate push rather than a gradual application.

Gravity and Freefall

Gravity is a force that pulls objects toward the ground, simulating real-world behavior. By default, most physics engines simulate gravity for all objects with rigidbody components. Gravity affects all game objects equally unless modified, and it is typically applied along the Y-axis (downward direction).

Here's an example of enabling gravity on an object in Unity:

```csharp
Copy code
void Start() {
    Rigidbody rb = GetComponent<Rigidbody>();
    rb.useGravity = true;
}
```

You can also adjust the gravity setting globally in your game engine to create unique environments. For instance, you can reduce gravity for a space-themed game or increase it to create a heavy, oppressive atmosphere.

Collision Detection

Collisions are vital in 3D games, as they determine when and how objects interact with each other. Whether it's a player colliding with walls or objects bumping into each other, collision detection is managed by the physics engine. To enable collisions, objects must have both a collider component and a rigidbody in Unity or similar components in other engines.

Here's an example of basic collision detection in Unity:

```csharp
Copy code
void OnCollisionEnter(Collision collision) {
    if (collision.gameObject.CompareTag("Enemy")) {
        Debug.Log("Collided with Enemy!");
    }
}
```

In this example, the OnCollisionEnter() function is triggered when the player collides with an object tagged as "Enemy," allowing for interactions such as damage, destruction, or a game over event.

Creating Movement Patterns (Jumping, Running, Flying)

In 3D games, player movement is one of the most engaging aspects. Jumping, running, and flying are common mechanics that can be implemented using a combination of transforms, forces, and physics.

Implementing Jumping

Jumping is often a core mechanic in platformers and action-adventure games. It involves applying an upward force to the player, counteracted by gravity pulling them back down. To ensure smooth and controlled jumps, it's important to check whether the player is on the ground before allowing another jump.

Here's how you can implement jumping in Unity:

```csharp
Copy code
public float jumpForce = 5f;
private bool isGrounded;

void Update() {
    if (isGrounded && Input.GetKeyDown(KeyCode.Space)) {
        Rigidbody rb = GetComponent<Rigidbody>();
        rb.AddForce(Vector3.up * jumpForce, ForceMode.Impulse);
```

```csharp
    }
}

void OnCollisionStay(Collision collision) {
    if (collision.gameObject.CompareTag("Ground")) {
        isGrounded = true;
    }
}

void OnCollisionExit(Collision collision) {
    if (collision.gameObject.CompareTag("Ground")) {
        isGrounded = false;
    }
}
```

In this code, the player can only jump when they are grounded, preventing mid-air jumps. The isGrounded variable is toggled based on whether the player is touching an object tagged as "Ground."

Implementing Running

Running typically involves increasing the player's movement speed when a specific input (such as holding down the shift key) is detected. Here's a simple way to implement running in Unity:

```csharp
csharp
Copy code
public float walkSpeed = 5f;
public float runSpeed = 10f;

void Update() {
    float moveSpeed = Input.GetKey(KeyCode.LeftShift) ? runSpeed
    : walkSpeed;

    float moveX = Input.GetAxis("Horizontal") * moveSpeed *
    Time.deltaTime;
    float moveZ = Input.GetAxis("Vertical") * moveSpeed *
    Time.deltaTime;
```

```
    transform.Translate(new Vector3(moveX, 0, moveZ));
}
```

When the player holds the shift key, their movement speed doubles, allowing them to run.

Implementing Flying

Flying introduces movement in all three dimensions (X, Y, and Z) without the restriction of gravity. It's often used in games with aerial or space-based mechanics.

Here's how you can implement basic flying mechanics in Unity:

```csharp
Copy code
public float flySpeed = 10f;

void Update() {
    float moveX = Input.GetAxis("Horizontal") * flySpeed *
    Time.deltaTime;
    float moveY = Input.GetAxis("FlyVertical") * flySpeed *
    Time.deltaTime;   // Fly up/down
    float moveZ = Input.GetAxis("Vertical") * flySpeed *
    Time.deltaTime;

    transform.Translate(new Vector3(moveX, moveY, moveZ));
}
```

In this case, the FlyVertical axis controls vertical movement (ascending and descending) while in flight.

Implementing Camera Controls: First-Person and Third-Person Views

Camera control is one of the most important elements of game design, as it directly impacts how players perceive and interact with the game world. Two common camera setups are first-person (where the camera shows the game from the player's point of view) and third-person (where the camera follows the player from behind or above).

First-Person Camera Controls

First-person cameras are typically used in games like shooters, exploration titles, and VR experiences. The camera is placed at the character's eye level, allowing players to see the world from the character's perspective.

Here's an example of first-person camera control in Unity:

```csharp
Copy code
public float mouseSensitivity = 100f;
public Transform playerBody;

void Start() {
    Cursor.lockState = CursorLockMode.Locked;
}

void Update() {
    float mouseX = Input.GetAxis("Mouse X") * mouseSensitivity *
    Time.deltaTime;
    float mouseY = Input.GetAxis("Mouse Y") * mouseSensitivity *
    Time.deltaTime;

    playerBody.Rotate(Vector3.up * mouseX);

    // Vertical rotation (up/down)
    transform.localRotation = Quaternion.Euler(-mouseY, 0f, 0f);
}
```

In this setup, the player can look around using the mouse, with horizontal movement rotating the player and vertical movement rotating the camera.

Third-Person Camera Controls

Third-person cameras are commonly used in action-adventure and RPG games. The camera follows the player character from behind or at an adjustable distance, offering a broader view of the surroundings.

Here's an example of third-person camera control in Unity:

```csharp
Copy code
public Transform player;
public Vector3 offset;
```

```
public float smoothSpeed = 0.125f;

void LateUpdate() {
    Vector3 desiredPosition = player.position + offset;
    Vector3 smoothedPosition = Vector3.Lerp(transform.position,
    desiredPosition, smoothSpeed);
    transform.position = smoothedPosition;

    transform.LookAt(player);
}
```

In this case, the camera smoothly follows the player, maintaining an offset distance, and continuously looks at the player to keep them centered in view.

In this chapter, we've covered the essential aspects of 3D object movement and rotation, from manipulating position, rotation, and scale to applying physics with forces, gravity, and collision detection. We've also explored how to implement various movement patterns like jumping, running, and flying, and how to control the camera in both first-person and third-person views. These techniques form the foundation for dynamic, interactive, and engaging gameplay in 3D games.

In the next chapter, we'll dive into user input and control systems, where we'll learn how players can interact with your game world using keyboard, mouse, and controllers.

Chapter 8: User Input and Control Systems

Introduction to User Input and Control Systems

In 3D games, user input is crucial for driving the gameplay experience. Whether it's moving a character, interacting with the environment, or controlling game mechanics, input systems translate player actions into responses within the game world. In this chapter, we will explore how to handle various types of input, from the basic keyboard and mouse setup to using game controllers. We will also cover how to make objects in a 3D space interactive and develop a simple character controller that allows players to navigate the game environment.

Setting Up Keyboard and Mouse Input

The keyboard and mouse are the most common input devices for PC-based games. They offer precise control over characters and interactions in the game, making them ideal for a variety of game genres, especially shooters, strategy games, and simulations. In this section, we will explore how to capture keyboard and mouse input, process it, and translate that input into actions within your 3D game.

Capturing Keyboard Input

To start with, let's look at how to capture keyboard input. Most game engines provide built-in support for detecting which keys are pressed and how to map them to game actions. For example, if you're using Unity, you can use the Input.GetKey() function to detect specific key presses. If you're using Unreal Engine, the input handling system allows you to bind keys to specific game actions directly in the project settings.

Here's a basic example of how to handle keyboard input in Unity:

```csharp
Copy code
void Update() {
    // Move forward
    if (Input.GetKey(KeyCode.W)) {
        transform.Translate(Vector3.forward * speed *
        Time.deltaTime);
    }

    // Move backward
    if (Input.GetKey(KeyCode.S)) {
        transform.Translate(Vector3.back * speed *
        Time.deltaTime);
    }

    // Rotate left
    if (Input.GetKey(KeyCode.A)) {
        transform.Rotate(Vector3.up, -rotationSpeed *
        Time.deltaTime);
    }

    // Rotate right
    if (Input.GetKey(KeyCode.D)) {
        transform.Rotate(Vector3.up, rotationSpeed *
        Time.deltaTime);
    }
}
```

In this example, the player uses the W, A, S, and D keys to move and rotate the character. The Input.GetKey() function checks whether a key is being held down, while the transform.Translate() and transform.Rotate() functions move the character in the appropriate direction.

Capturing Mouse Input

In addition to the keyboard, the mouse is often used to control camera movement and interact with objects in the game. For example, in a first-person shooter, the mouse is commonly used to control where the player is looking, and mouse clicks are used to interact with the environment or trigger events (like shooting or selecting objects).

Mouse input typically involves capturing the movement of the mouse and mapping it to changes in the camera's rotation. Here's a simple example of how to control camera rotation with the mouse in Unity:

```csharp
Copy code
public float mouseSensitivity = 100f;
public Transform playerBody;
private float xRotation = 0f;

void Start() {
    Cursor.lockState = CursorLockMode.Locked;
}

void Update() {
    float mouseX = Input.GetAxis("Mouse X") * mouseSensitivity *
    Time.deltaTime;
    float mouseY = Input.GetAxis("Mouse Y") * mouseSensitivity *
    Time.deltaTime;

    xRotation -= mouseY;
    xRotation = Mathf.Clamp(xRotation, -90f, 90f); // Limit
    vertical rotation to avoid over-rotation

    playerBody.Rotate(Vector3.up * mouseX);
    transform.localRotation = Quaternion.Euler(xRotation, 0f, 0f);
}
```

In this code, the Input.GetAxis() function captures mouse movement along the X and Y axes, which is then used to rotate the camera. The Cursor.lockState = CursorLockMode.Locked line locks the cursor to the center of the screen, ensuring that mouse movement translates into smooth camera control, which is crucial for first-person games.

Customizing Input Settings

Most game engines allow you to customize input settings, letting players remap keys or adjust sensitivity. In Unity, this is done through the Input Manager, where you can define custom input axes and assign them to specific actions in the game. Unreal Engine offers a similar setup, where input bindings can be configured in the project settings or via Blueprint nodes for more advanced control schemes.

It's important to remember that giving players the option to remap keys and adjust sensitivity improves accessibility and user experience, making your game more flexible for different playstyles and preferences.

Controller Input in 3D Games

While keyboard and mouse are prevalent in PC gaming, many players prefer using game controllers for their tactile and intuitive feel, especially in action games, racing games, and sports simulations. Controllers often feature analog sticks, triggers, and buttons, providing a different input dynamic compared to traditional keyboard and mouse setups.

Setting Up Controller Input

Setting up controller input is relatively straightforward in most modern game engines, as they offer built-in support for common game controllers like Xbox or PlayStation controllers. These controllers come with a standard set of inputs, including analog sticks for movement, triggers for actions, and buttons for various commands.

In Unity, controller input can be managed using the same Input.GetAxis() function that handles mouse movement. For example, the left analog stick can be used to control player movement, while the right stick controls the camera. Here's an example:

```csharp
Copy code
void Update() {
    float moveX = Input.GetAxis("Horizontal") * speed *
    Time.deltaTime;
    float moveZ = Input.GetAxis("Vertical") * speed *
    Time.deltaTime;

    Vector3 move = transform.right * moveX + transform.forward *
```

```
    moveZ;
    controller.Move(move);
}
```

In this case, the Horizontal and Vertical axes map to the left analog stick's X and Y input, which are used to move the player. Similarly, the triggers can be mapped to actions like jumping or shooting:

```
csharp
Copy code
if (Input.GetButtonDown("Jump")) {
    // Execute jump action
}
```

Mapping Controls for Different Platforms

One of the challenges of developing a game that supports multiple platforms is ensuring that input controls feel intuitive on both keyboard/mouse setups and game controllers. This often involves creating separate input schemes for each platform and offering in-game options that allow players to switch between input methods seamlessly.

When designing controller input, it's essential to consider factors like the layout of the buttons, the feel of the analog sticks, and how each control method complements the gameplay. For instance, racing games tend to map acceleration and braking to the controller's triggers, while action-adventure games may use the analog stick for movement and the buttons for jumping and interacting.

Interaction with 3D Objects (Clicking, Picking Up)

In 3D games, interacting with objects in the game world is an essential feature. Players need to be able to pick up objects, trigger events, or examine items by clicking or using an interact button. These interactions are typically achieved through raycasting—a technique where a ray is cast from the camera (or player) into the 3D scene, detecting whether it intersects with any objects.

Implementing Raycasting for Object Interaction

Raycasting is an efficient way to detect objects that the player is aiming at. In a first-person game, for example, you can cast a ray from the center of the camera's viewpoint to determine if the player is looking at an object they can interact with. Here's an example of how to implement raycasting in Unity:

```csharp
Copy code
void Update() {
    if (Input.GetMouseButtonDown(0)) {
        Ray ray =
        Camera.main.ScreenPointToRay(Input.mousePosition);
        RaycastHit hit;

        if (Physics.Raycast(ray, out hit)) {
            if (hit.collider.CompareTag("Interactable")) {
                InteractWithObject(hit.collider.gameObject);
            }
        }
    }
}

void InteractWithObject(GameObject obj) {
    // Code to interact with the object (e.g., pick it up, open a
    door)
}
```

In this example, when the player clicks the mouse, a ray is cast from the camera to the point where the mouse cursor is located on the screen. If the ray hits an object with the tag "Interactable," the InteractWithObject() function is called, allowing the player to interact with that object.

Picking Up and Moving Objects

In some games, such as puzzle games or physics-based simulations, players may need to pick up and manipulate objects within the game world. This can be achieved by attaching the object to the player's hand or a holding point using physics-based interactions.

Here's an example of how to pick up and carry objects in Unity:

```csharp
Copy code
public Transform holdPoint;

void Update() {
    if (Input.GetMouseButtonDown(0)) {
        Ray ray =
        Camera.main.ScreenPointToRay(Input.mousePosition);
        RaycastHit hit;

        if (Physics.Raycast(ray, out hit)) {
            if (hit.collider.CompareTag("Pickable")) {
                PickUpObject(hit.collider.gameObject);
            }
        }
    }
}

void PickUpObject(GameObject obj) {
    obj.transform.position = holdPoint.position;
    obj.transform.parent = holdPoint;
}
```

In this code, when the player clicks on an object tagged as "Pickable," the object is moved to a predefined hold point and becomes a child of that point, following the player's movements. Releasing the object can be implemented by detaching it from the parent and allowing it to fall back into the game world.

Developing a Simple Character Controller

A character controller is one of the most fundamental systems in any 3D game, as it dictates how the player moves and interacts with the environment. In this section, we will develop a simple character controller that allows the player to walk, run, and jump through the game world.

Character Movement

A basic character controller handles forward, backward, and lateral movement, as well as jumping. Here's an example of how to create a simple character controller in Unity:

```csharp
Copy code
public CharacterController controller;
public float speed = 12f;
public float gravity = -9.81f;
public float jumpHeight = 3f;
private Vector3 velocity;

void Update() {
    float moveX = Input.GetAxis("Horizontal");
    float moveZ = Input.GetAxis("Vertical");

    Vector3 move = transform.right * moveX + transform.forward *
    moveZ;
    controller.Move(move * speed * Time.deltaTime);

    if (Input.GetButtonDown("Jump") && controller.isGrounded) {
        velocity.y = Mathf.Sqrt(jumpHeight * -2f * gravity);
    }

    velocity.y += gravity * Time.deltaTime;
    controller.Move(velocity * Time.deltaTime);
}
```

In this controller, the player moves based on input from the Horizontal and Vertical axes, and the CharacterController component is used to handle collisions and movement. The gravity is applied to the player to simulate realistic physics, and jumping is implemented by calculating the required velocity to achieve a certain jump height.

Adding Additional Features

You can expand on this basic character controller by adding additional features like sprinting, crouching, or even climbing. By combining keyboard and mouse input with controller input, you can offer a seamless experience for players, allowing them to feel in full control of the character's movements.

Chapter 9: Building 3D Game Environments

Introduction to Building 3D Game Environments

The environment of a 3D game shapes the player's experience, serving as both a backdrop and a key element in gameplay. Whether you're crafting vast, open-world landscapes or tightly controlled interior spaces, the design of a game world plays a crucial role in storytelling, immersion, and player engagement. In this chapter, we will explore the process of designing 3D game environments, from large-scale terrain generation to fine details like asset placement and environmental effects. We will also cover the use of skyboxes to enhance the visual atmosphere, ultimately guiding you through the creation of believable and captivating game worlds.

Designing a Game World: Scale and Realism

When designing a game world, it's essential to balance scale and realism. Large, expansive worlds can offer players a sense of freedom and exploration, while smaller, more contained environments might lend themselves to focused, story-driven gameplay. Regardless of the scale, the key to successful environment design lies in creating a world that feels believable within the context of the game.

Scale: How Big Should the Game World Be?

The scale of your game world depends on the type of game you're developing. Open-world games, for instance, typically require vast environments for players to explore, whereas linear games may only need tightly designed levels. To determine the appropriate scale for your game, consider the following factors:

- **Gameplay mechanics**: Does your game require open exploration, or is it more focused on tight, mission-based gameplay? Open-world games need large, interconnected spaces, while puzzle or action games might benefit from smaller, more detailed environments.
- **Storytelling needs**: If your game's story spans across different locations, you'll need a larger environment. On the other hand, a focused narrative might take place in a single location, reducing the need for expansive areas.
- **Player progression**: How will the player move through the world? A game that offers vehicles or fast travel might benefit from a larger world, while games with slower-paced movement might need a more condensed space.

In an open-world game like *The Legend of Zelda: Breath of the Wild*, the vastness of the environment encourages exploration and discovery. In contrast, a game like *Portal* uses smaller, highly controlled environments to guide the player through puzzles and narrative beats.

Realism: Achieving Believability in the Game World

Realism in game environments doesn't always mean replicating the real world exactly, but rather creating a world that feels coherent and believable within the game's context. Even in fantasy or science fiction games, consistency in design helps immerse players in the world. To achieve realism:

- **Use real-world references**: Study real-world environments similar to the ones in your game. Take note of how geography, architecture, and natural elements interact in the real world, then adapt them to fit your game's needs.
- **Consider player movement and interaction**: Ensure that the scale and design of your environment make sense with how players move and

interact. For example, if your player character can jump high or move quickly, you'll need to design your environment to accommodate that.

- **Balance between detail and performance**: While adding detail enhances realism, be mindful of performance constraints. Overloading a scene with high-detail assets can affect game performance, so focus on optimizing assets and using techniques like level of detail (LOD) to balance detail and performance.

Terrain Generation and Sculpting Tools

Terrain generation is a critical aspect of creating large, natural landscapes in 3D games. Instead of manually designing every hill, valley, and river, terrain generation tools allow you to quickly create complex landscapes that can be customized and refined using sculpting techniques. These tools help speed up the process while maintaining control over the final look of the terrain.

Procedural Terrain Generation

Procedural terrain generation is a method of creating landscapes algorithmically, often using fractals or noise functions like Perlin noise. This technique is popular in games with large, open-world environments because it allows developers to generate vast, varied landscapes with minimal manual input. In games like *Minecraft* or *No Man's Sky*, procedural generation is used to create endless worlds, ensuring that no two environments are the same.

Here's a basic example of using procedural terrain generation in Unity:

```csharp
Copy code
void GenerateTerrain() {
    Terrain terrain = GetComponent<Terrain>();
    TerrainData terrainData = terrain.terrainData;
    int width = terrainData.heightmapResolution;
    int height = terrainData.heightmapResolution;

    float[,] heights = new float[width, height];
```

```
for (int x = 0; x < width; x++) {
    for (int y = 0; y < height; y++) {
        heights[x, y] = Mathf.PerlinNoise(x * 0.05f, y *
        0.05f);
    }
}
terrainData.SetHeights(0, 0, heights);
}
```

In this example, we use Perlin noise to generate height values for the terrain, creating a landscape with smooth hills and valleys. Adjusting the frequency of the noise allows for more or less rugged terrain.

Sculpting Tools

Sculpting tools offer a more hands-on approach to terrain creation. Most game engines, like Unity and Unreal Engine, come with built-in terrain sculpting tools that allow developers to paint heightmaps, smooth terrain, and add details like cliffs or plateaus. This technique provides greater control over the shape and layout of the environment compared to purely procedural generation.

Here are a few key features of sculpting tools:

- **Raise/Lower Terrain**: This tool allows you to push and pull the terrain, raising it to create hills or mountains and lowering it to create valleys or depressions.
- **Smooth Terrain**: After manipulating the terrain, the smooth tool helps blend rough edges, ensuring that transitions between different heights look natural.
- **Paint Terrain Textures**: Many sculpting tools let you apply textures to specific areas of the terrain, such as grass, dirt, or rock, helping to create realistic-looking surfaces.

Combining Procedural Generation and Sculpting

One effective way to design complex game environments is to combine procedural generation with manual sculpting. Use procedural generation to create the base landscape, then refine specific areas by hand using sculpting tools. This approach allows for the best of both worlds: the speed and efficiency of procedural generation, coupled with the creative control of manual sculpting.

Placing Assets and Creating Natural Landscapes

Once your terrain is sculpted and shaped, the next step is to populate the environment with assets like trees, rocks, buildings, and other natural or man-made objects. Proper asset placement is essential to creating a natural, believable environment, as random or thoughtless placement can make your world feel artificial.

Using Asset Placement Tools

Game engines often provide asset placement tools to help streamline the process of placing objects in the world. These tools allow for quick placement of multiple objects with randomized positioning, rotation, and scale to make them feel natural. For example, Unity's terrain editor includes a tree and detail painting tool that lets you paint trees, grass, and rocks onto the terrain like a brushstroke.

Here's a breakdown of key asset placement considerations:

- **Randomization**: When placing assets like trees or rocks, slight variations in position, rotation, and scale can make the environment feel more natural. Manually adjusting each asset can be time-consuming, so many tools offer randomization options to help automate this process.
- **Density**: Natural environments often feature varied densities of objects. For example, forests might have dense clusters of trees in some areas and sparse growth in others. Adjusting the density of assets based on terrain features (such as placing more trees on flatter areas and fewer on steep slopes) adds a layer of realism to the environment.
- **Layering**: Layering assets creates a sense of depth and complexity. For example, a natural landscape might include trees as the primary layer, followed by smaller plants and bushes, with rocks or fallen logs scattered

throughout as additional details.

Hand-Placing Key Landmarks

While randomization tools are great for populating large areas quickly, key landmarks should be placed manually to ensure they stand out. Landmarks could include unique rock formations, buildings, bridges, or other important structures that guide the player's attention or provide points of interest in the world.

For example, in *The Elder Scrolls V: Skyrim*, landmarks like towering mountains or ancient ruins are strategically placed to draw the player's eye and encourage exploration.

Using Skyboxes and Environmental Effects

Skyboxes and environmental effects play a significant role in setting the mood and atmosphere of your game world. A skybox is essentially a large, textured cube or sphere that surrounds the environment, simulating the sky, clouds, distant mountains, or space. In addition to skyboxes, environmental effects like fog, rain, snow, and lighting changes can further enhance the realism and immersion of your game environment.

Creating and Applying Skyboxes

Skyboxes are typically created as a set of six images, one for each face of a cube (up, down, left, right, front, and back). These images are stitched together to form a seamless background that gives the illusion of a distant horizon.

In Unity, applying a skybox is as simple as selecting a pre-made skybox material or creating your own. You can even animate skyboxes to simulate time passing, with the sky changing from day to night.

Here's how you can apply a skybox in Unity:

```
csharp
Copy code
```

```
void Start() {
    RenderSettings.skybox = daySkyboxMaterial;
}
```

Skyboxes can greatly impact the tone of your game. For example, a bright, clear sky with fluffy clouds creates a cheerful and optimistic atmosphere, while a dark, stormy sky sets a more ominous and foreboding mood.

Environmental Effects

Environmental effects like weather, lighting, and post-processing filters can add another layer of realism to your game world. Here are a few examples of common environmental effects:

- **Fog**: Fog can be used to create atmosphere and limit the player's visibility, adding a sense of mystery or danger to certain areas.
- **Weather**: Rain, snow, or wind can add dynamic elements to your environment. Games like *The Witcher 3* use weather systems to change the feel of the world, with storms making the environment feel hostile and foreboding.
- **Lighting**: Time-of-day lighting changes, dynamic shadows, and sun-shafts can create a more immersive environment. For instance, early morning light might cast long shadows and soft rays, while midday lighting is bright and harsh.
- **Post-Processing**: Effects like bloom, motion blur, and color correction can enhance the visual style of your game world. Subtle color adjustments can change the overall tone, making an environment feel warmer or colder depending on the scene.

Building 3D game environments is an intricate process that combines technical skills with artistic vision. From designing the overall scale and realism of the world to using terrain generation and sculpting tools, asset placement, and environmental effects, each element contributes to the player's sense of immersion. A well-designed environment not only supports gameplay mechanics but also enhances the storytelling and emotional impact of the game.

In the next chapter, we will explore lighting and shading techniques in 3D games, learning how to create dynamic, atmospheric lighting that enhances the visual appeal and realism of your game environment.

Chapter 10: Level Design Principles

I ntroduction
Level design is where gameplay, art, and story intersect, shaping
the player's experience as they navigate the game world. Whether
you're creating fast-paced action sequences, complex puzzle rooms, or
vast open-world environments, the structure and layout of your levels are
crucial to keeping players engaged. Effective level design requires a balance
between guiding the player's journey, introducing challenges, and providing
opportunities for exploration. This chapter will explore the core principles of
level design, from structuring game levels and adding obstacles to designing
for exploration and providing tips for efficiency.

Structuring Game Levels: Progression and Challenges

The structure of a game level determines how players move through it, how
challenges unfold, and how they experience progression. The flow of a
level should be intuitive, with a clear beginning, middle, and end, while
also offering a balance between difficulty and reward. Well-structured
levels make the game feel engaging and provide players with a sense of
accomplishment as they overcome challenges and move forward.

Progression: Building a Sense of Growth

Level progression is about more than just moving from one area to another.
It's about building a sense of growth and achievement in the player. As
they progress through the game, players should feel like they're becoming
stronger, more skilled, or more knowledgeable. This is often achieved by

gradually increasing the difficulty of challenges, introducing new gameplay mechanics, and rewarding players with new abilities or items.

- **Start simple, grow complex**: Early levels should introduce basic mechanics in a controlled way, allowing players to learn the game's core systems without overwhelming them. As players advance, levels should introduce new challenges or variations of existing mechanics that require the player to think and act more strategically.
- **Pacing is key**: It's essential to balance periods of intense action with moments of calm or exploration. Too many high-stress moments in a row can lead to player fatigue, while too many calm moments can make the game feel slow or boring. Good pacing alternates between the two, providing breaks and opportunities for reflection or discovery between challenging sequences.
- **Milestones and rewards**: Dividing a level into smaller milestones gives players a sense of accomplishment. This can be done through checkpoints, mini-bosses, or unique challenges that signal progress. Rewards like new weapons, abilities, or in-game currency also reinforce the feeling of growth and provide motivation to continue.

For example, in *Super Mario Bros.*, levels gradually introduce new obstacles and enemies, allowing players to build confidence before facing more complex challenges. This progression keeps the player engaged while ensuring the difficulty curve feels fair and rewarding.

Challenges: Creating a Balance of Difficulty

Challenges are at the heart of level design. Whether they take the form of puzzles, enemies, or physical obstacles, the key is to provide enough challenge to engage players without making the game frustratingly difficult. Good challenges feel fair and offer players the chance to succeed through skill, strategy, or ingenuity.

- **Risk and reward**: Players should feel like taking risks can lead to rewards. Placing valuable items or shortcuts in difficult-to-reach areas encourages players to push their limits and try new strategies. However, these rewards should be optional so that players who prefer a safer approach can still progress.

- **Variety in challenges**: Repetitive challenges can make a level feel tedious. Introduce variety by changing up the types of obstacles, enemies, or puzzles players encounter. This keeps gameplay fresh and prevents players from falling into a predictable rhythm.
- **Learning through failure**: Design challenges in a way that players can learn from their mistakes. Instead of punishing players harshly for failure, offer them the chance to understand what went wrong and try again with a different approach. This can be achieved through well-placed checkpoints or providing visual and auditory cues that hint at the correct solution.

Adding Obstacles and Enemies

Obstacles and enemies are essential elements that create tension and excitement in a level. They push players to test their skills and develop strategies to overcome the challenges they face. The design and placement of obstacles and enemies play a major role in shaping the difficulty and flow of the level.

Designing Obstacles

Obstacles can take many forms, from environmental hazards like pits and spikes to locked doors or puzzles that require a solution to proceed. The goal is to create obstacles that feel like natural parts of the game world and require players to think creatively to overcome them.

- **Physical obstacles**: These include things like gaps, moving platforms, or dangerous terrain. They challenge the player's reflexes and platforming skills. Physical obstacles should be visible and clearly telegraphed, giving players time to react and avoid failure.
- **Interactive obstacles**: Interactive obstacles, such as switches, levers, or buttons, often require players to solve puzzles or use specific mechanics

to progress. These obstacles are great for breaking up combat-heavy sections of the game, offering players a mental challenge instead of a physical one.

- **Timed obstacles**: Adding time-based challenges, such as doors that close after a certain period or moving platforms that require precise timing, can increase tension and force players to think on their feet. However, these should be used sparingly to avoid frustration.

Placing Enemies

Enemies add another layer of challenge to levels by forcing players to engage in combat, stealth, or avoidance. Enemy placement should be deliberate and varied, creating moments of tension and excitement without overwhelming the player.

- **Enemy variety**: A diverse range of enemies keeps combat encounters interesting. Some enemies might attack head-on, while others provide support from a distance or use special abilities that require unique strategies to defeat.
- **Strategic placement**: Placing enemies in strategic locations can make a level more challenging and engaging. For example, placing archers on high ledges forces the player to be cautious and look for cover, while placing melee enemies in narrow hallways limits the player's ability to dodge and creates more intense close-quarters combat.
- **Scaling difficulty**: As the player progresses, enemies should become more challenging, either by increasing their numbers, improving their abilities, or introducing entirely new enemy types. However, this increase in difficulty should feel natural and gradual, rather than overwhelming.

A classic example of effective enemy placement is seen in *Dark Souls*. Enemies are often positioned to surprise or ambush the player, creating moments of high tension. However, the game also allows players to observe enemy behavior and plan their approach, rewarding careful strategy over brute force.

Designing for Player Exploration

Exploration is a key part of many 3D games, giving players the freedom to discover hidden areas, collectibles, and lore that expand the game world. Well-designed levels encourage players to explore by offering rewards and interesting sights just off the beaten path, while still maintaining a clear main route for those who prefer a more straightforward experience.

Encouraging Exploration

To make exploration rewarding, it's important to give players a reason to deviate from the main path. Hidden collectibles, secret areas, or optional side quests can provide players with additional challenges and rewards.

- **Visual cues**: Use visual cues to hint at hidden areas or secret paths. A partially obscured door, a trail of coins, or a crack in the wall can subtly suggest that there's more to discover if the player investigates further.
- **Reward curiosity**: Exploration should feel rewarding, whether through tangible items like health upgrades or more abstract rewards like learning more about the game's lore. Even if the player finds nothing but a beautiful view, that moment of discovery can be a reward in itself.
- **Non-linear level design**: While it's important to maintain a clear sense of direction for the player, non-linear level design encourages exploration by offering multiple paths or branching routes. Players can choose how they want to navigate the level, which can create a more personalized experience.

Managing Player Freedom

While exploration is rewarding, it's essential not to overwhelm players with too much freedom. A good level design strikes a balance between allowing players to explore and guiding them toward the main objective. This can be achieved through:

- **Subtle guidance**: Use lighting, color contrast, or unique landmarks to subtly guide the player toward key objectives. For example, a brightly lit doorway at the end of a dark corridor naturally draws the player's attention without feeling forced.
- **Gating progression**: Introduce barriers that the player must overcome before progressing, such as locked doors that require keys or areas that are only accessible after the player obtains a new ability. This technique ensures that the player doesn't stray too far from the intended path while still offering opportunities for exploration.

In games like *The Legend of Zelda: Breath of the Wild*, the player is free to explore almost the entire world from the beginning. However, certain areas are designed to be more challenging than others, subtly encouraging the player to follow a specific progression path while still allowing for the freedom to explore.

Tips for Efficient Level Design

Designing levels efficiently is a skill that comes with practice and careful planning. A well-structured workflow can save time, reduce frustration, and ensure that your levels are polished and engaging. Here are some tips to help streamline the level design process:

Plan Before You Build

Before jumping into the editor, take time to plan out your level. Sketch a rough map of the layout, noting important areas, obstacles, and enemy encounters. Consider the flow of the level and how you want the player to progress. By having a clear vision from the start, you can avoid wasting time on unnecessary revisions.

Block Out the Level First

Before adding details, create a rough version of the level using simple geometry (often called a "blockout" or "graybox"). This allows you to focus on the layout, flow, and mechanics without getting bogged down in details. Once the blockout feels right, you can begin adding more complex assets, textures, and lighting.

Playtest Early and Often

Regular playtesting is essential to ensure your level is fun, balanced, and free of frustrating elements. Playtest the level yourself and ask others to test it as well. Watching someone else play your level can reveal issues you might not have noticed, such as unclear objectives or difficulty spikes.

Iterate and Refine

Level design is an iterative process. Don't be afraid to make changes based on playtesting feedback. Sometimes even small tweaks, like adjusting the placement of a platform or changing the timing of an obstacle, can significantly improve the player's experience.

Level design is one of the most critical aspects of creating a successful 3D game. By structuring levels with clear progression, introducing balanced challenges, and encouraging exploration, you can create immersive and engaging game worlds that keep players coming back for more. Efficient design practices, like planning ahead and playtesting frequently, ensure that your levels are polished and enjoyable.

In the next chapter, we'll explore how to optimize performance in your 3D game, ensuring that your levels run smoothly on a variety of hardware without sacrificing quality.

Chapter 11: Implementing Artificial Intelligence (AI)

I ntroduction to AI in Games
  Artificial Intelligence (AI) in video games is the engine that drives the behaviors and decisions of non-player characters (NPCs) and enemies, making the game world feel dynamic and responsive. Whether it's a guard patrolling a hallway, an enemy chasing the player, or a shopkeeper interacting with the player's character, AI helps to create immersive and challenging gameplay experiences. The role of AI in games is to simulate real-world intelligence and behaviors while balancing complexity and performance.

The implementation of AI varies significantly across genres. In a 3D game, AI can govern the way enemies move through the environment, react to the player's actions, and strategize during combat. It can also be used to create realistic NPCs that follow daily routines or react dynamically to the player's presence. AI is not just about enemies—it enhances the richness of the game world, creating interactions that keep players engaged and challenged.

This chapter will dive into various aspects of AI in 3D game development, including popular pathfinding algorithms, the use of behavior trees and finite state machines (FSMs) for enemy AI, and how to create meaningful interactions with NPCs.

Pathfinding Algorithms (A*, NavMesh)

Pathfinding is a core element of AI in games, enabling characters to navigate the game environment intelligently. It's the foundation that allows enemies to chase the player, NPCs to move around, and characters to avoid obstacles. Two of the most widely used pathfinding algorithms in 3D games are **A*** and **NavMesh** (Navigation Mesh).

A* Algorithm: The Basics

A* (pronounced "A-star") is a popular pathfinding algorithm known for its efficiency in navigating complex environments. It calculates the shortest path from one point (usually the character's starting position) to another (the destination) while avoiding obstacles. A* works by searching through a graph of possible paths, weighing each path by its cost—often defined by distance or difficulty of traversal.

- *How A Works**: A* combines two values to determine the cost of a path:
- **G-cost**: The actual movement cost from the starting point to the current position.
- **H-cost**: The estimated cost from the current position to the destination (this is often the straight-line distance).
- The algorithm continually selects the path with the lowest combined G-cost and H-cost, exploring the most efficient routes first.
- **Advantages of A***: The strength of A* lies in its precision. It always finds the shortest path, given that there is one, and can navigate around complex obstacles. This makes it suitable for scenarios where AI characters need to navigate confined spaces, like buildings or mazes.

However, A* can be computationally expensive in large, open-world environments. The more complex the terrain, the longer the algorithm takes to compute a path. Therefore, A* is ideal for smaller areas where precise movement is required.

NavMesh: Navigation for Open Worlds

For larger, more dynamic 3D environments, **NavMesh** is a better alternative. A NavMesh is a data structure that represents the walkable areas of the game world. Instead of calculating paths in real time like A*, NavMesh predefines which areas are navigable, allowing AI to move freely within these zones.

- **How NavMesh Works**: The game world is divided into convex polygons, and AI characters move from polygon to polygon, selecting the most direct path between them. NavMesh algorithms take into account obstacles, slopes, and uneven terrain, ensuring that AI characters avoid areas they can't traverse.
- **Dynamic NavMesh**: In dynamic environments where obstacles or terrain can change during gameplay (e.g., collapsing bridges or moving platforms), dynamic NavMesh can update the walkable zones in real-time, preventing characters from getting stuck or lost.

NavMesh is efficient in open-world games, providing smooth navigation across vast landscapes. It's used in many AAA titles, including *The Witcher 3* and *Assassin's Creed*, where characters need to move seamlessly through cities, forests, and mountains without recalculating paths constantly.

Choosing Between A* and NavMesh

The choice between A* and NavMesh depends on the scope of your game's environments. For tight, indoor spaces with complex layouts, A* offers precision, making it ideal for AI that needs to navigate corridors or rooms. On the other hand, for large, open-world games, NavMesh provides efficient navigation across varied terrains.

Enemy AI: Behavior Trees and Finite State Machines

Creating intelligent enemies requires more than just pathfinding. AI needs to simulate decision-making and adapt to the player's actions. Two common approaches to enemy AI in 3D games are **Behavior Trees** and **Finite State Machines (FSMs)**. These techniques allow you to define how enemies react to stimuli, pursue goals, and switch between different behaviors.

Behavior Trees

Behavior trees are a popular way of structuring AI behaviors because they provide a modular, scalable approach to decision-making. In a behavior tree, an AI character's actions are represented as nodes in a tree structure. Each node represents a decision or action, and the tree flows from top to bottom, executing actions based on predefined conditions.

- **Root Node**: The starting point of the tree. The AI checks the root node first before moving on to other decisions.
- **Composite Nodes**: These are decision-making nodes that dictate the flow of the tree. For example, a "sequence" node will execute a series of actions in order, while a "selector" node will choose one action from a list of options.
- **Leaf Nodes**: These are the actual actions the AI performs, such as attacking, moving, or patrolling.

Behavior trees are flexible and easy to expand, making them ideal for complex enemy AI. You can break down behaviors into small, manageable parts and build upon them without needing to rewrite the entire system. For example, you could create a simple behavior tree where an enemy patrols until it sees the player, then switches to attacking.

- **Example of a Behavior Tree**:
- **Root Node**: Patrol -> Detect Player
- **Selector Node**:
- If Player Detected -> Chase
- If in Attack Range -> Attack
- If Player Escapes -> Resume Patrol

This modular structure allows for easy modification, such as adding new conditions or behaviors (e.g., searching for the player after losing sight of them).

Finite State Machines (FSM)

Finite State Machines (FSMs) are another approach to enemy AI. In an FSM, an enemy AI can only be in one state at any given time (e.g., idle, attacking, fleeing), and it switches between these states based on inputs or conditions. Each state has specific behaviors, and transitions between states occur when certain criteria are met.

- **States**: A finite set of conditions (e.g., patrol, alert, attack). An enemy can only be in one state at a time.
- **Transitions**: Conditions that trigger a switch from one state to another (e.g., when the player enters the enemy's line of sight, the enemy switches from "patrol" to "chase").
- **Actions**: Behaviors associated with each state (e.g., when in the "attack" state, the enemy performs an attack animation and reduces the player's health).

FSMs are simpler than behavior trees but can be just as effective for certain types of AI. They are especially useful for predictable enemy behaviors, such as guard patrols or boss fight mechanics. However, FSMs can become difficult to manage if you need to implement a large number of states and transitions, making them less scalable than behavior trees.

- **Example of FSM for Enemy AI**:
- **State 1**: Idle (Patrol Route)
- **Transition 1**: If Player Detected -> Switch to "Chase"
- **State 2**: Chase (Move Towards Player)
- **Transition 2**: If in Attack Range -> Switch to "Attack"
- **State 3**: Attack (Engage Player)
- **Transition 3**: If Player Escapes -> Switch to "Search" or "Idle"

FSMs are ideal for straightforward AI behaviors, especially when the number of possible states is limited.

Non-Player Character (NPC) Interaction

While enemies often take center stage in AI discussions, **NPC interactions** are equally important, especially in RPGs, open-world games, and story-driven experiences. NPCs populate the game world, providing players with quests, dialogue, and opportunities to interact with the environment. Designing believable, engaging NPCs requires more than just scripting responses—it requires a system that adapts to the player's actions and creates dynamic interactions.

Dialogue Systems

One of the most common ways players interact with NPCs is through dialogue. A well-designed dialogue system can make NPCs feel more lifelike and create deeper player engagement. There are several approaches to dialogue in games, ranging from linear scripts to more complex, branching conversations that respond to player choices.

- **Branching Dialogue Trees**: These are common in RPGs and story-heavy games, where the player's choices in dialogue can affect the outcome of the conversation or even the game world. For example, in *Mass Effect*, player choices during conversations affect relationships with NPCs and the direction of the story.
- **Dynamic Responses**: To create more reactive NPCs, use a system that allows NPCs to respond dynamically to the player's actions or status. For instance, if the player has completed a major quest, NPCs could comment on their success. This adds a layer of realism and immersion to the game world.

NPC Behavior and Routines

Creating NPCs that feel like they're part of a living world involves more than just dialogue. NPCs should have behaviors and routines.

Optimizing AI Performance

As your game scales and the number of AI-controlled characters increases, performance becomes a critical factor. Poorly optimized AI can lead to significant frame rate drops, affecting the overall gameplay experience. This section will delve into strategies for optimizing AI performance, ensuring that your game runs smoothly without sacrificing the intelligence and responsiveness of your AI systems.

Profiling AI Performance

Before implementing optimizations, it's essential to profile your AI systems to identify performance bottlenecks. Profiling tools can help you understand where the CPU spends most of its time and which AI components are consuming the most resources.

- **Tools for Profiling**: Many game engines come with built-in profiling tools. For example, Unity has the Profiler window, which allows you to track CPU and GPU usage, memory allocation, and more. Unreal Engine provides similar tools for analyzing performance metrics. Use these tools to gather data on AI calculations during gameplay, especially in scenarios with many active AI agents.
- **Identifying Bottlenecks**: Look for spikes in CPU usage or long execution times in your AI logic. Pay particular attention to pathfinding calculations and decision-making processes. If specific areas of your game cause performance issues, consider isolating those sections for deeper analysis.

Reducing Update Frequencies

One effective method for optimizing AI performance is to reduce the frequency of updates for non-critical AI characters. Not every AI character needs to evaluate its behavior every frame. Instead, you can implement various update strategies based on the importance and proximity of the AI to the player.

- **Distance-Based Updates**: For AI that is far from the player or not currently engaged, consider reducing the update frequency. For example, an enemy on patrol who is out of the player's sight can check for the player's presence every few seconds instead of every frame. You might set a threshold distance, and if an AI character is outside this threshold, it only updates its state periodically.
- **Event-Driven Updates**: Rather than continuously checking conditions, use events to trigger updates when certain actions occur. For instance, if an AI character is alerted by a sound, it can then start evaluating its behavior. This approach helps reduce the CPU load by eliminating unnecessary calculations.

Spatial Partitioning

In complex 3D environments, managing how AI characters perceive and interact with the world is crucial for performance. **Spatial partitioning** techniques can help reduce the number of checks an AI character must perform by dividing the game world into smaller, manageable sections.

- **Quadtree and Octree**: These data structures divide the game world into sections (2D for quadtree, 3D for octree) based on the spatial distribution of objects. AI characters can quickly query which section of the world they are in and only check for interactions with other characters and objects in that section. This reduces the overhead of checking every AI against every other object in the world.
- **Grid-Based Partitioning**: This approach involves dividing the game world into a grid of cells. Each AI character can determine its current cell and only interact with other characters within the same or adjacent cells. This method is particularly effective in games with large environments where characters are unlikely to interact with distant objects.

Caching and Reusing AI Calculations

Another optimization strategy involves caching results of expensive calculations. If certain AI actions or pathfinding calculations produce results that are likely to be reused, storing these results can save processing time.

- **Caching Pathfinding Results**: When an AI character successfully calculates a path, cache the result. If the character needs to navigate to the same destination again without changes in the environment, it can reuse the cached path instead of recalculating it. Implementing a time limit for cached paths can help maintain responsiveness in dynamic environments.
- **Using State Caching**: For AI that switches between states, consider caching results for each state. For instance, if an enemy detects a player and transitions from patrolling to chasing, cache the results of any calculations relevant to the chase. When the enemy switches back to patrolling, it can return to its last known state quickly without recalculating everything.

Level of Detail (LOD) for AI

Implementing Level of Detail (LOD) for AI can also optimize performance. Just as graphics engines reduce the complexity of 3D models at a distance, AI can simplify behavior as it moves farther from the player.

- **Simplified AI Logic**: For AI characters that are far away, use simplified versions of their decision-making processes. For example, instead of using a full behavior tree for distant enemies, you might implement a basic patrol behavior with limited detection capabilities. This reduces the computational burden on the CPU while maintaining a believable world.
- **Adaptive AI Complexity**: Adjust the complexity of AI behavior based on the player's distance or engagement level. If an enemy is alerted and actively chasing the player, it may utilize its full behavior tree. However, if the player is out of sight or the enemy is idle, switch to a simpler logic that consumes fewer resources.

Optimizing AI performance is essential for delivering an enjoyable gaming experience. By profiling your AI systems, reducing update frequencies, utilizing spatial partitioning, caching calculations, and applying LOD techniques, you can significantly improve your game's performance without sacrificing the complexity and responsiveness of AI behaviors.

In the next chapter, we will explore the intricacies of **game state management**—how to handle transitions between different game states, including menus, gameplay, and game over screens, ensuring a smooth user experience. Game state management is a vital component that ties together various elements of your game and enhances player engagement.

Chapter 12: Particle Systems and Special Effects

P article systems and special effects are essential components of modern 3D game development. They enhance the visual experience, providing depth and realism to game environments. This chapter delves into the intricacies of particle systems, explores various special effects like fire, smoke, and weather phenomena, and offers guidance on optimizing performance. We will also examine how to script events for special effects to create dynamic and engaging gameplay experiences.

Introduction to Particle Systems

Particle systems are used to simulate a variety of phenomena in games, such as fire, smoke, explosions, and other effects that consist of many small particles. These systems allow developers to create complex visual effects efficiently without requiring the rendering of detailed geometry for each individual particle.

Understanding Particle Systems

A particle system is a collection of many small images or sprites (particles) that represent physical entities like flames, smoke, or debris. These particles are typically managed and rendered by a specialized engine that handles their properties, behavior, and rendering. The key attributes of particle systems include:

1. **Lifetime**: Each particle has a defined lifespan, which determines how long it remains visible before disappearing. This attribute is crucial for simulating effects like smoke dissipating or flames flickering.
2. **Emission Rate**: The rate at which particles are generated. A higher emission rate can create more intense effects, such as a roaring fire or a violent explosion.
3. **Velocity**: The initial speed and direction of particles. This attribute helps in creating realistic motion, such as the upward flicker of flames or the downward drift of ash.
4. **Color and Transparency**: Particles can change color and transparency over their lifetime, allowing for dynamic visual effects. For instance, smoke may start dark and become lighter as it dissipates.
5. **Size**: The size of each particle can change over its lifetime. This can create the illusion of depth and dimension in effects like smoke or fire.

Common Particle Effects

Particle systems can simulate various effects, each with unique characteristics:

1. **Fire**: Fire particles typically have a bright color palette, including oranges, yellows, and reds. They often flicker, change size, and move upward to simulate the natural behavior of flames.
2. **Smoke**: Smoke effects usually involve gray or black particles that billow and spread. These particles are often semi-transparent and have varying sizes, creating a sense of volume and depth.
3. **Explosions**: Explosions can combine multiple particle types, including debris, smoke, and fire. The initial burst can be bright and loud, followed by a cloud of smoke and scattered debris.
4. **Magic Effects**: Particles can also represent magical spells or effects in fantasy games. These particles often have vibrant colors and may

119

include sparkles, glows, or trails to emphasize their otherworldly nature.

5. **Weather Effects**: Particle systems can simulate environmental effects like rain, snow, or fog. These systems often involve large numbers of small particles that create a cohesive visual experience.

Basic Structure of a Particle System

At its core, a particle system consists of several components:

1. **Emitter**: The source of particles, which defines the location, shape, and emission rate of the particles. Emitters can take various forms, including point emitters, box emitters, or even meshes.
2. **Particle Properties**: The attributes that define how particles behave, including lifetime, size, color, and velocity.
3. **Update Logic**: The code responsible for updating the state of each particle each frame, including their position, color, and size based on their properties.
4. **Rendering Logic**: The process of drawing particles on the screen, usually done using sprites or textured quads. This involves considering the camera perspective and ensuring proper blending and transparency effects.
5. **Collision Detection**: In some cases, particle systems need to interact with the game environment. Implementing collision detection can enable particles to respond to obstacles or other game entities.

Creating Water, Fog, and Weather Effects

In addition to fire and explosions, particle systems can be used to create various atmospheric effects that enrich the game environment. Water, fog, and weather effects are integral in establishing mood and realism in games.

Creating Water Effects

Water effects can range from calm lakes to raging rivers and splashes from rain or swimming characters. While particle systems play a role in simulating splashes, ripples, and foam, more complex techniques may be needed for realistic water surfaces.

Techniques for Water Effects

1. **Splash Particles**: When a character jumps into water, creating splash particles can enhance the realism. Emit particles in the shape of a cone to simulate the water being displaced.
2. **Ripple Effects**: Implementing ripple effects requires careful manipulation of particle behavior. Particles should propagate outward from the point of impact, gradually fading away.
3. **Foam and Bubbles**: To add realism to water surfaces, integrate foam and bubble particles. Foam particles should be semi-transparent and have a shorter lifespan, creating a dynamic look.
4. **Reflections and Refractions**: While not strictly part of the particle system, utilizing shaders can enhance water effects by simulating reflections and refractions, giving depth to the water surface.

Creating Fog Effects

Fog can create atmosphere and depth in game environments, making them feel more expansive or mysterious. Fog particles are typically semi-transparent and may vary in size and density.

Techniques for Fog Effects

1. **Layered Fog**: Create multiple layers of fog with varying densities to simulate depth. Adjust the opacity of each layer to create a more realistic appearance.
2. **Movement**: Implement subtle movement to fog particles to prevent them from feeling static. This can be achieved by applying a slow,

random velocity to the fog particles.

3. **Color Variation**: Introduce slight color variations in fog particles to simulate different types of fog. For example, a dense, swampy fog may have a greenish hue, while a cold, misty fog may appear bluish.

4. **Fog Volume**: Utilize volumetric fog techniques, which can provide a more realistic effect than traditional particle systems. This involves rendering a fog volume rather than individual particles, creating a more cohesive look.

Creating Weather Effects

Weather effects, such as rain and snow, can significantly enhance the gameplay experience. Particle systems are commonly used to simulate these effects, adding realism and immersion.

Techniques for Rain Effects

1. **Rain Particles**: Create thin, elongated particles to represent raindrops. Adjust their velocity and lifetime to simulate the falling motion.

2. **Splash Effects**: When raindrops hit surfaces, creating splash effects can enhance realism. Emit splash particles from the point of impact, simulating the water displacement.

3. **Wind Direction**: Implement wind direction by adjusting the trajectory of rain particles. This can add realism to rain by simulating environmental conditions.

4. **Puddles and Accumulation**: For a more advanced effect, implement puddles that form as rain accumulates. This requires a combination of particle effects and terrain manipulation.

Techniques for Snow Effects

1. **Snow Particles**: Create soft, white particles that fall slowly to represent snowflakes. Adjust their size and opacity to simulate different snow types.

2. **Accumulation**: Implement snow accumulation on surfaces by creating particles that stick to objects over time, creating a dynamic winter environment.

3. **Blizzard Effects**: For blizzards, increase the density of snow particles and add wind effects to create the illusion of strong winds blowing snow around.

4. **Snow Trails**: If characters or objects interact with the snow, consider implementing snow trails that visually represent movement through the snow.

Optimizing Performance for Special Effects

While particle systems can create stunning visuals, they can also be resource-intensive. Optimizing performance is crucial to maintain a smooth gameplay experience, especially in resource-limited environments.

Techniques for Performance Optimization

1. **Particle Count Management**: Limit the maximum number of particles emitted by a system at any given time. Use techniques such as particle pooling to reuse particles instead of creating new ones.

2. **Culling**: Implement frustum culling to avoid rendering particles outside the camera's view. This can significantly reduce the rendering workload.

3. **Level of Detail (LOD)**: Use LOD techniques for particle systems. Create different particle representations based on distance from the camera, reducing the detail for distant particles while maintaining higher quality up close.

4. **Batching**: Group similar particles together for rendering. Batching reduces the number of draw calls, improving performance by minimizing the overhead associated with switching between different materials.

5. **Shader Optimization**: Use efficient shaders for rendering particles. Avoid complex calculations in the fragment shader and utilize texture

atlases to reduce the number of texture bindings.

6. **Simulation Resolution**: Adjust the simulation resolution for particle systems. For instance, if a system creates thousands of particles but only a few are visible, lowering the resolution can save resources.

Profiling and Testing

1. **Performance Profiling**: Use profiling tools available in game engines to identify bottlenecks in your particle systems. Analyze performance metrics and optimize the most resource-intensive parts of your systems.

2. **Testing on Multiple Platforms**: Test performance on various hardware configurations to ensure that particle systems run smoothly across a range of devices. This helps identify potential issues that may arise on less powerful systems.

Scripting Events for Special Effects

Scripting is an essential aspect of integrating particle systems and special effects into gameplay. By leveraging scripting, developers can create dynamic and interactive environments that respond to player actions and events.

Event-Driven Special Effects

Event-driven special effects are triggered by specific in-game actions or conditions. For example, an explosion may occur when a player triggers a specific event, such as destroying an object.

Techniques for Event Scripting

1. **Event Listeners**: Implement event listeners that respond to player actions or game events. These listeners can trigger the appropriate particle effects when certain conditions are met.

2. **Trigger Zones**: Use trigger zones in the game world to initiate particle effects. When a player enters a designated area, the corresponding

effects can activate, enhancing immersion.

3. **State Machines**: For more complex interactions, consider implementing state machines that govern particle systems. This approach allows for intricate behavior changes based on game states.

4. **Combining Effects**: Integrate multiple particle systems to create complex events. For example, when a player detonates a bomb, simultaneously trigger fire, smoke, and debris effects to create a more impactful visual.

Scripting Examples

Here are some examples of how to implement scripting for special effects:

Example 1: Triggering an Explosion

When a player interacts with an explosive object, you can trigger an explosion particle system:

```javascript
Copy code
function onExplosiveInteraction() {
    // Trigger explosion particle system
    explosionParticleSystem.emit();

    // Optionally, trigger sound effects
    playExplosionSound();
}
```

Example 2: Creating a Smoke Trail

For a character that uses a jetpack, you can script a smoke trail that appears when the jetpack is activated:

```javascript
Copy code
function update() {
    if (isJetpackActive) {
        smokeParticleSystem.emitAt(character.position);
```

```
    }
}
```

Combining Particle Systems with Game Logic

Integrating particle systems with game logic enhances the interactivity of your game. For instance, you can use particle effects to indicate when a player is low on health or when a special ability is activated.

Example 3: Health Indicators

When a player's health drops below a certain threshold, you can trigger a visual effect to signify danger:

```javascript
Copy code
if (player.health < threshold) {
    dangerParticleSystem.emitAt(player.position);
}
```

Particle systems and special effects are integral to creating immersive and visually stunning 3D games. By understanding how to implement and optimize these systems, developers can enhance the gameplay experience, making their worlds feel alive and dynamic. As you continue your journey in 3D game programming, experimenting with different effects and refining your particle systems will empower you to bring your creative visions to life. In the following chapters, we will explore advanced techniques and tools that will further elevate your game development skills, ensuring you can craft experiences that captivate players from the moment they enter your game world.

Chapter 13: Physics Engines and Simulations

P hysics engines are vital components in game development that bring realism and interactivity to 3D environments. They simulate real-world physics behaviors, allowing objects to move, collide, and react in ways that mimic the physical properties of the real world. In this chapter, we will explore advanced physics concepts in games, collision detection and handling, simulating real-world effects, and building destructible environments.

Advanced Physics in Games

Rigidbody and Kinematic Objects

At the heart of most physics engines are two primary types of objects: **Rigidbody** and **Kinematic**. Understanding the distinction between these types is essential for developing realistic and interactive gameplay.

- **Rigidbody**: A Rigidbody is an object that is influenced by forces and can collide with other objects. It responds to gravity, applies forces, and reacts to collisions, making it ideal for simulating real-world physics. In Unity, for instance, a Rigidbody component allows the game object to be affected by physics simulations. This enables behaviors such as falling, bouncing, and sliding.

- **Kinematic**: Kinematic objects, on the other hand, are not affected by physics forces. They move through code and can interact with other objects, but they do not react to physics. This is useful for objects that need to move in a predetermined way, such as platforms that slide back and forth or characters that need to navigate the environment without being influenced by gravity or external forces.

Choosing Between Rigidbody and Kinematic

When deciding whether to use a Rigidbody or a Kinematic object, consider the intended behavior and interaction of the object within the game. If an object needs to respond dynamically to collisions and environmental forces, it should be a Rigidbody. However, if precise control is required without the influence of physics, such as a character controller or moving platform, a Kinematic object is more suitable.

Combining Rigidbodies and Kinematic Objects

In many cases, games will have a combination of both Rigidbody and Kinematic objects. For example, a character might have a Kinematic controller to manage movement while interacting with Rigidbodies (like walls or floors) in the environment. This allows developers to create fluid and responsive gameplay experiences, as the Kinematic object can determine its position while still being affected by the physics of other objects.

Collision Detection and Handling

Collision detection is crucial for creating believable interactions between objects in a game world. The physics engine must determine when two objects collide and how to handle that collision.

Types of Collision Detection

There are two main types of collision detection: **Discrete** and **Continuous**.

- **Discrete Collision Detection**: This method checks for collisions at fixed intervals, such as once per frame. It is efficient and works well for most cases but may miss fast-moving objects that pass through each other between frames. For example, if a projectile moves quickly enough, it could skip over a target without registering a hit.
- **Continuous Collision Detection**: This method calculates the trajectory of an object and checks for collisions along the entire path it takes during the frame. Continuous detection is more computationally intensive but prevents the tunneling problem where fast-moving objects pass through one another without detection. It is ideal for fast-moving objects such as bullets or cars.

Collision Handling

Once a collision is detected, the physics engine needs to determine how to handle it. There are several approaches to collision resolution:

- **Elastic Collisions**: In an elastic collision, both momentum and kinetic energy are conserved. This means that when two objects collide, they bounce off each other without losing speed. This is common in ball games where players expect objects to bounce realistically.
- **Inelastic Collisions**: In inelastic collisions, momentum is conserved, but kinetic energy is not. Objects may stick together upon impact or crumple, leading to a loss of energy. This is often seen in car crashes where vehicles may come to a stop or deform upon impact.
- **Restitution**: The restitution property of a collision determines how "bouncy" an object is. A restitution value of 1 means a perfectly elastic collision, while a value of 0 means a perfectly inelastic collision. By adjusting restitution values, developers can control how objects behave

after collisions.

Simulating Real-World Effects

To create a convincing 3D game world, it is essential to simulate various real-world effects such as gravity, friction, and bouncing.

Gravity

Gravity is one of the fundamental forces that should be simulated in a 3D game. Most physics engines provide a global gravity setting that can be adjusted for the entire scene. For example, Unity uses a standard gravity value of -9.81 m/s², which mimics Earth's gravity.

- **Custom Gravity**: Developers can create custom gravity settings for specific objects or environments. For instance, a platformer game might have lower gravity to enable higher jumps, while a space simulation might have zero gravity to allow for free movement in a spacecraft.

Friction

Friction is the force that resists the relative motion of two surfaces in contact. It is crucial for creating realistic interactions between objects.

- **Static vs. Dynamic Friction**: Static friction occurs when two surfaces are not moving relative to each other, while dynamic friction comes into play when they are sliding. In game development, developers can specify friction coefficients for materials to simulate different surfaces—such as slick ice or rough asphalt—impacting how characters or objects move across them.
- **Adjusting Friction**: Most physics engines allow developers to adjust friction properties for colliding objects. By fine-tuning these values, developers can create realistic movement dynamics that enhance gameplay

experiences. For example, characters may slide more on icy surfaces while gripping tightly on rough terrain.

Bouncing

Simulating bouncing effects is important for objects like balls, projectiles, or any elements in your game that require elastic interactions.

- **Controlling Bounciness**: Using the restitution property mentioned earlier, developers can fine-tune how much objects bounce after collisions. By setting different restitution values for various surfaces, you can create interesting gameplay mechanics. A rubber ball might bounce high on a concrete surface while a wooden block barely rebounds on the same surface.
- **Particle Effects**: In addition to the physics simulation, adding particle effects such as dust or debris when an object hits the ground can further enhance the realism of bouncing effects. This creates visual feedback that complements the physics simulation and provides players with a more immersive experience.

Building Destructible Environments

Creating destructible environments adds an extra layer of interactivity and realism to games. Players appreciate being able to influence their surroundings, whether it's blowing up a wall, knocking down a tree, or smashing objects in the environment.

Approaches to Destruction

There are various methods for implementing destructible environments, and the choice often depends on the complexity and scale of the game.

- **Pre-Fractured Models**: One common method involves creating pre-fractured models that separate into pieces when destroyed. For example, a wall can be modeled in such a way that it splits into smaller chunks upon impact. This technique is relatively easy to implement and allows for quick destruction effects without complex calculations.

- **Procedural Fracturing**: For more advanced destruction, procedural fracturing can be employed. This method involves dynamically breaking objects apart based on the forces applied during gameplay. Physics engines can calculate how an object should fracture in real-time, leading to more realistic and unpredictable destruction patterns.

- **Destruction Libraries**: Many game engines and third-party libraries offer built-in tools for creating destructible environments. For example, the Unity Asset Store has assets that simplify the process of creating destructible objects, while Unreal Engine includes advanced tools for simulating destruction through the Chaos Physics engine.

Considerations for Performance

While destructible environments add excitement to gameplay, they can also be performance-intensive. It's essential to manage the complexity of destruction systems to maintain a smooth player experience.

- **Level of Detail (LOD)**: Implementing LOD techniques for destructible objects can help optimize performance. For example, as players move further away from destructible objects, switch to lower-resolution models to reduce the computational load.

- **Pooling System**: Using a pooling system for destroyed objects can also enhance performance. Instead of instantiating new objects every time a structure is destroyed, you can reuse existing destroyed fragments and enable or disable them as needed. This reduces memory allocation and improves performance during gameplay.

Feedback and Visual Effects

Creating visually appealing feedback for destruction enhances the player experience. Consider incorporating:

- **Particle Effects**: Adding particle effects like debris, dust clouds, or smoke can create a more immersive experience when an object is destroyed. These effects help convey the impact of destruction to the player.
- **Sound Effects**: Sound design is equally important. Adding appropriate sound effects for destruction, such as cracking wood or shattering glass, reinforces the realism of the environment and makes interactions more satisfying.
- **Camera Shake**: Implementing camera shake effects during significant destruction events can enhance the dramatic impact. This technique adds a layer of immersion and excitement, making players feel the weight of their actions within the game world.

In this chapter, we explored the crucial role of physics engines and simulations in game development. We discussed advanced concepts such as Rigidbody and Kinematic objects, collision detection and handling, and simulating real-world effects like gravity, friction, and bouncing. Additionally, we delved into the complexities of building destructible environments, balancing realism and performance.

The implementation of physics in games significantly enhances player experience by creating a dynamic and responsive world. In the next chapter, we will focus on sound design in games—exploring how to effectively incorporate audio elements to elevate gameplay and enrich the gaming atmosphere. Sound design is a powerful tool for immersing players and conveying the emotional weight of their actions, making it an essential aspect of game development.

Chapter 14: Adding Sound and Music

Sound and music play a pivotal role in the overall experience of 3D games. They can evoke emotions, enhance immersion, and provide crucial feedback to players. This chapter will delve into the importance of audio in 3D games, discuss implementing background music and sound effects, explore the concept of 3D spatial audio, and examine how audio can be used to enhance gameplay.

Importance of Audio in 3D Games

Creating Immersion

One of the primary functions of sound in gaming is to create a sense of immersion. Just as visual elements draw players into a game world, audio can make that world feel more alive. The sound of footsteps crunching on gravel, the rustling of leaves, or distant thunder can all transport players into the environment. Without these auditory cues, a game may feel flat or lifeless, reducing the overall impact on the player.

Emotional Engagement

Audio also plays a critical role in emotional engagement. The right music can enhance the emotional weight of a scene, whether it's the tension of an impending battle or the serenity of a peaceful moment. Soundtracks that adapt to gameplay can make players feel more connected to their character and the narrative, heightening their emotional response. For example, a dramatic score may swell during a pivotal cutscene, making players feel the stakes of the story.

Providing Feedback

In addition to immersion and emotional impact, audio provides essential feedback. Sound effects alert players to actions and events in the game, helping them understand what is happening in real time. The sound of a weapon firing, a door creaking open, or an enemy approaching can guide players' decisions and actions. Well-designed audio cues can also indicate success, failure, or important transitions, enhancing gameplay flow.

Enhancing Storytelling

Audio elements can significantly enhance storytelling. Voice acting, for instance, can bring characters to life, allowing players to form connections and empathy with them. Music can underscore pivotal moments, enriching the narrative experience. By integrating audio effectively, developers can convey themes and emotions that visuals alone may struggle to communicate.

Implementing Background Music and Sound Effects

Background Music

Implementing background music requires careful consideration of genre, mood, and pacing. Here's how to effectively integrate music into your game:

1. **Choosing the Right Genre**: The genre of music should align with the game's theme. A fantasy adventure may benefit from orchestral scores, while a sci-fi game might require electronic or synth-based music. Understanding the emotional landscape of your game will help you select the appropriate genre.

2. **Dynamic Music Systems**: Implementing a dynamic music system allows the soundtrack to adapt to gameplay. For instance, the music can shift in intensity during combat or calm down when exploration is happening. This responsiveness can enhance player engagement and create a more immersive experience.

3. **Looping and Transitions**: Background music should loop seamlessly to prevent disruptions. Consider transitions between different music tracks, such as changing from exploration music to combat music. Using crossfading techniques can create smooth transitions that keep the player engaged.

4. **Volume Control**: It's essential to balance the volume of the background music with sound effects and dialogue. Music should enhance the experience without overwhelming other audio elements. Providing players with audio settings can allow them to customize their experience.

Sound Effects

Sound effects (SFX) add a layer of realism and interactivity to the game. Here are some best practices for implementing sound effects:

1. **Creating a Sound Library**: Developing a library of sound effects specific to your game can streamline the process. This library can include footsteps, environmental sounds, and interactions with objects. Quality sound effects that match the aesthetics of the game will enhance immersion.

2. **Layering Sounds**: For complex actions, layering multiple sound effects can create a richer auditory experience. For example, when a character jumps, layering the sound of a jump with the impact of landing can create a more convincing audio experience.

3. **Spatial Sound Effects**: Implementing spatial sound effects can enhance realism by simulating how sound behaves in the real world. For instance, the sound of a gunshot should feel different depending on the player's distance from the source.

4. **Environmental Sounds**: Adding ambient sounds helps to flesh out the game world. Background noise such as birds chirping, water flowing, or wind rustling can create a more immersive atmosphere. This ambient audio can help reinforce the setting and tone of the game.

5. **Sound Design for Interactions**: Design sound effects for specific interactions to provide feedback. For instance, if a player picks up an item, a distinctive sound cue can indicate success. These audio cues help players feel a sense of accomplishment and guide their actions.

3D Spatial Audio: Positioning Sound in 3D Space

Understanding Spatial Audio

3D spatial audio refers to the technique of placing sound in a three-dimensional space around the player. This approach enhances realism by allowing players to perceive sound directionally, just as they would in the real world. When a sound source is positioned correctly in 3D space, players can instinctively know whether a sound is coming from behind, in front, or above them.

Implementing Spatial Audio

To implement spatial audio effectively in a 3D game, consider the following:

1. **Positioning Sound Sources**: Assign sound sources to specific objects or events within the game world. For example, the sound of footsteps should originate from the character's location, while ambient sounds can be placed throughout the environment to create an immersive audio experience.

2. **Attenuation**: As sound travels through space, it naturally diminishes in volume. Implementing attenuation curves can simulate how sound fades over distance. This is especially important for ensuring that sounds feel natural, rather than abruptly cutting off when a player

moves away from a sound source.

3. **Doppler Effect**: The Doppler effect is the change in frequency or wavelength of sound in relation to an observer moving relative to the source of the sound. For example, as a car approaches and passes by, the pitch of the engine sound changes. Integrating this effect can add realism to fast-moving objects in the game.

4. **3D Sound APIs**: Many game engines, such as Unity and Unreal Engine, provide built-in support for spatial audio through specialized audio APIs. These APIs enable developers to create rich audio experiences by managing sound positioning, volume, and attenuation.

5. **Testing and Iteration**: Testing spatial audio in various gameplay scenarios is crucial. Ensure that players can accurately locate sound sources and that the audio enhances the overall experience. Gathering feedback during playtesting can help identify areas for improvement.

Using Audio to Enhance Gameplay

Audio as Gameplay Feedback

Sound effects can provide players with vital feedback about their actions, guiding them through the gameplay experience. Here's how audio can enhance gameplay:

1. **Contextual Cues**: Different audio cues can signal various gameplay contexts. For example, the sound of a sword clashing can indicate combat, while a subtle ambient sound can signal exploration. By using unique sound cues, players can understand their environment and make informed decisions.

2. **Reinforcing Game Mechanics**: Audio can reinforce game mechanics by providing feedback for player actions. For example, a satisfying sound when collecting an item can enhance the feeling of accomplishment, while a distinct failure sound can signal mistakes.

3. **Encouraging Exploration**: Sound can encourage players to explore

the game world. Subtle audio cues may lead players to hidden areas or important objects. For instance, distant music may attract players to a hidden quest location, creating a sense of discovery.

Using Music to Signal Events

Background music can be used to signal key events or transitions in gameplay. Consider these techniques:

1. **Event-Driven Music**: Use music to enhance important events, such as boss battles, cutscenes, or significant narrative moments. The music should adapt to the intensity of the situation, increasing the emotional impact of the moment.
2. **Dynamic Changes**: Create dynamic changes in music based on player actions. For example, if players enter a combat zone, the music can shift from calm exploration to an intense battle theme. This can signal to players that they need to prepare for challenges ahead.
3. **Mood and Theme Matching**: Ensure that the music matches the mood and theme of the gameplay. For example, lighthearted music may accompany comedic moments, while dramatic music may underline tense situations. Properly aligned audio will amplify the desired emotional response from players.

Balancing Audio Elements

Balancing various audio elements is crucial for maintaining an enjoyable experience. Here are some best practices for audio balancing:

1. **Volume Control**: Offer players options to adjust volume levels for music, sound effects, and dialogue. This allows players to customize their experience and ensures that no audio element overwhelms another.
2. **Playtesting**: Conduct thorough playtesting to gather feedback on audio

levels. Pay attention to player reactions and adjust volumes based on their responses to ensure a balanced and enjoyable audio experience.

3. **Consistency**: Maintain consistency in audio design throughout the game. Using a cohesive sound palette can help unify the audio experience and enhance immersion. This includes consistent use of effects, voice acting, and musical themes.

4. **Audio Cues for Game Progression**: Implement audio cues that signal progress or transitions in gameplay. For example, a sound cue may indicate when a player completes a level or unlocks a new ability, reinforcing the sense of achievement.

In this chapter, we explored the critical role of audio in 3D games, emphasizing its importance in creating immersion, emotional engagement, and gameplay feedback. We discussed how to implement background music and sound effects, the significance of spatial audio, and techniques for enhancing gameplay through audio.

Sound and music are not mere complements to the visual experience; they are integral elements that can define a game's identity and evoke powerful emotional responses. By thoughtfully integrating audio into the game design, developers can create a richer, more immersive experience that resonates with players long after they've put down the controller. In the following chapter, we will explore the art of optimizing audio performance in your game, ensuring that your soundscapes remain as engaging and impactful as possible.

Chapter 15: Scripting Game Logic

G ame scripting is the backbone of interactive game development. It defines how game objects behave, how player inputs are processed, and how the overall game experience is managed. This chapter will explore the intricacies of scripting game logic, focusing on the use of popular game scripting languages such as JavaScript and C#. We'll cover writing core game functions, managing game states, and integrating events with code, providing you with a comprehensive understanding of how to bring your game to life through scripting.

Introduction to Game Scripting Languages

Game scripting languages serve as the bridge between game design and programming, allowing developers to implement gameplay mechanics without delving deep into the underlying engine code. While many game engines come with their own scripting languages, others support widely-used languages such as JavaScript and C#.

JavaScript

JavaScript is a versatile and powerful language primarily used for web development, but it has gained traction in game development, especially with frameworks like Phaser and libraries like Three.js for 3D games. Its ability to run in browsers makes it an ideal choice for creating web-based games.

Advantages of JavaScript

1. **Ease of Use**: JavaScript has a syntax that is relatively easy to learn and understand, making it accessible for beginners.
2. **Dynamic and Flexible**: JavaScript is dynamically typed and can adapt to various programming styles, enabling rapid development.
3. **Rich Ecosystem**: A vast array of libraries and frameworks can simplify game development, including libraries for physics, animation, and user interfaces.
4. **Cross-Platform Compatibility**: Games developed in JavaScript can run on any device with a modern web browser, allowing for easy distribution and access.

Disadvantages of JavaScript

1. **Performance**: While JavaScript is performant for many applications, it can be slower than compiled languages like C#, especially for CPU-intensive tasks.
2. **Security**: Since JavaScript runs in browsers, it can be more vulnerable to security issues like code injection.

C#

C# is a powerful, statically typed language that is widely used in game development, particularly with the Unity game engine. C# provides robust performance, making it a popular choice for both 2D and 3D games.

Advantages of C#

1. **Strong Typing**: C#'s static typing can help catch errors during compilation, reducing runtime bugs.
2. **Performance**: C# generally offers better performance than JavaScript for more complex calculations, making it suitable for larger game projects.

3. **Rich Feature Set**: C# includes features like garbage collection, which can help manage memory automatically, reducing memory leaks.
4. **Integration with Unity**: C# is the primary scripting language for Unity, providing a wealth of resources, documentation, and community support.

Disadvantages of C#

1. **Learning Curve**: C# can be more challenging to learn than JavaScript for complete beginners, especially due to its more complex features.
2. **Platform Dependency**: C# is not as universally supported as JavaScript, as it is primarily used in conjunction with the .NET framework and specific game engines.

Writing Core Game Functions

Core game functions form the foundation of gameplay, dictating how the game operates, how characters move, how scores are calculated, and more. Writing these functions requires a solid understanding of the game's mechanics and how players interact with them.

Basic Structure of Game Functions

Game functions typically follow a common structure, which includes:

1. **Function Definition**: Each function is defined with a name, parameters, and a return type. For example, a function to move a character might look like this in C#:

```
csharp
Copy code
```

```
void MoveCharacter(float speed, Vector3 direction) {
    transform.position += direction * speed * Time.deltaTime;
}
```

1. **Parameters**: Functions can accept parameters that dictate how they behave. In the example above, speed and direction influence how the character moves.
2. **Return Values**: Some functions may return values, such as scores or states. This allows for dynamic interactions based on gameplay conditions.

Core Game Functions Examples

1. Player Movement

One of the most fundamental functions in a game is player movement. Here's how you might implement player movement in both JavaScript and C#.

JavaScript Example:

```javascript
Copy code
function movePlayer(player, speed) {
    if (keys.up) {
        player.y -= speed;
    }
    if (keys.down) {
        player.y += speed;
    }
    if (keys.left) {
        player.x -= speed;
    }
    if (keys.right) {
        player.x += speed;
    }
```

```
}
```

C# Example:

```csharp
csharp
Copy code
void Update() {
    float speed = 5.0f;
    Vector3 direction = new Vector3(Input.GetAxis("Horizontal"),
    Input.GetAxis("Vertical"), 0);
    MoveCharacter(speed, direction);
}
```

2. Score Calculation

Calculating and updating the score based on player actions is another essential function.

JavaScript Example:

```javascript
javascript
Copy code
let score = 0;

function updateScore(points) {
    score += points;
    console.log("Score: " + score);
}
```

C# Example:

```csharp
csharp
Copy code
int score = 0;

void UpdateScore(int points) {
    score += points;
```

```
    Debug.Log("Score: " + score);
}
```

Implementing Game Logic

The true power of scripting comes from the ability to integrate multiple functions into cohesive gameplay logic. Here's an example of combining movement and scoring:

JavaScript Example:

```javascript
javascript
Copy code
function updateGame() {
    movePlayer(player, playerSpeed);
    if (playerCollidesWithEnemy(player)) {
        updateScore(-10);
    }
}
```

C# Example:

```csharp
csharp
Copy code
void Update() {
    MoveCharacter(speed, GetInputDirection());
    if (CheckCollisionWithEnemy()) {
        UpdateScore(-10);
    }
}
```

Game States: Menus, Levels, End Screens

Managing game states is crucial for providing a seamless user experience. Game states define different stages in the game, such as the main menu, gameplay, pause screens, and end screens.

Defining Game States

Game states can be represented using enumerations in C# or simple constants in JavaScript. This makes it easy to manage transitions between states.

C# Example:

```
csharp
Copy code
public enum GameState {
    MainMenu,
    Playing,
    Paused,
    GameOver
}

private GameState currentState = GameState.MainMenu;
```

JavaScript Example:

```
javascript
Copy code
const GameState = {
    MAIN_MENU: 'mainMenu',
    PLAYING: 'playing',
    PAUSED: 'paused',
    GAME_OVER: 'gameOver'
};

let currentState = GameState.MAIN_MENU;
```

147

Managing Game States

Switching between states involves checking the current state and executing corresponding logic. Here's how you can manage game states.

JavaScript Example:

```javascript
javascript
Copy code
function update() {
    switch (currentState) {
        case GameState.MAIN_MENU:
            displayMainMenu();
            break;
        case GameState.PLAYING:
            updateGame();
            break;
        case GameState.PAUSED:
            displayPauseMenu();
            break;
        case GameState.GAME_OVER:
            displayGameOverScreen();
            break;
    }
}
```

C# Example:

```csharp
csharp
Copy code
void Update() {
    switch (currentState) {
        case GameState.MainMenu:
            DisplayMainMenu();
            break;
        case GameState.Playing:
            UpdateGame();
            break;
        case GameState.Paused:
```

```
        DisplayPauseMenu();
        break;
    case GameState.GameOver:
        DisplayGameOverScreen();
        break;
    }
}
```

Transitioning Between States

Implementing functions for transitioning between game states allows for smooth gameplay and user interface management.

JavaScript Example:

```javascript
javascript
Copy code
function startGame() {
    currentState = GameState.PLAYING;
    initializeGame();
}

function pauseGame() {
    currentState = GameState.PAUSED;
}

function gameOver() {
    currentState = GameState.GAME_OVER;
}
```

C# Example:

```csharp
csharp
Copy code
void StartGame() {
    currentState = GameState.Playing;
    InitializeGame();
```

```
}

void PauseGame() {
    currentState = GameState.Paused;
}

void GameOver() {
    currentState = GameState.GameOver;
}
```

Integrating Game Events with Code

Game events are crucial for creating an engaging gameplay experience. They define how the game responds to player actions, environmental changes, and other dynamic elements.

Understanding Game Events

Game events can be triggered by various actions, such as player inputs, collisions, timers, or even external signals like network messages in multiplayer games.

Event Types

1. **Input Events**: Triggered by player actions, such as pressing keys or clicking the mouse.
2. **Collision Events**: Occur when game objects interact, such as a player colliding with an enemy.
3. **Timer Events**: Triggered after a specified duration, allowing for actions like spawning enemies or creating power-ups.
4. **Custom Events**: Developers can create specific events tailored to their game's mechanics.

Implementing Event Listeners

Event listeners are functions that respond to specific events. Here's how to implement them in both JavaScript and C#.

JavaScript Example:

```javascript
Copy code
document.addEventListener('keydown', function(event) {
    if (event.key === 'p') {
        pauseGame();
    }
});
```

C# Example:

```csharp
Copy code
void Start() {
    InputManager.OnPausePressed += PauseGame;
}
```

Triggering Events

Triggering events involves calling event listeners or functions when specific conditions are met.

JavaScript Example:

```javascript
Copy code
function updateGame() {
    if (playerCollidesWithEnemy(player)) {
        triggerGameOver();
    }
```

```
}
```

C# Example:

```csharp
csharp
Copy code
void Update() {
    if (CheckCollisionWithEnemy()) {
        TriggerGameOver();
    }
}
```

Example: Complete Event Integration

Here's an example that ties everything together, illustrating how game events can interact with game states and core functions.

JavaScript Example:

```javascript
javascript
Copy code
function updateGame() {
    if (currentState === GameState.PLAYING) {
        movePlayer(player, playerSpeed);
        if (playerCollidesWithEnemy(player)) {
            triggerGameOver();
        }
    }
}

function triggerGameOver() {
    currentState = GameState.GAME_OVER;
    displayGameOverScreen();
}
```

C# Example:

```csharp
Copy code
void Update() {
    if (currentState == GameState.Playing) {
        MoveCharacter(speed, GetInputDirection());
        if (CheckCollisionWithEnemy()) {
            TriggerGameOver();
        }
    }
}

void TriggerGameOver() {
    currentState = GameState.GameOver;
    DisplayGameOverScreen();
}
```

Scripting game logic is an essential skill for game developers. By mastering game scripting languages like JavaScript and C#, you can create engaging gameplay experiences that respond dynamically to player actions. Understanding how to write core game functions, manage game states, and integrate events with code will empower you to build games that are not only functional but also enjoyable. With practice, you'll be able to leverage these skills to craft your own unique game mechanics, ensuring your projects stand out in a competitive landscape.

As you continue your journey in game development, remember that scripting is a blend of creativity and technical skill. Embrace the challenges and experiment with different approaches to find what works best for your projects. Happy coding!

Chapter 16: Game Optimization and Performance

I n the realm of game development, creating visually stunning and immersive experiences is only part of the equation. Ensuring that games run smoothly and efficiently is crucial for maintaining player engagement and satisfaction. This chapter focuses on various techniques and strategies for optimizing game performance, including reducing lag and increasing frame rates, implementing Level of Detail (LOD) techniques, managing memory effectively, and optimizing for different platforms such as PC, mobile, and console.

Reducing Lag and Increasing Frame Rate

Lag and low frame rates can severely detract from the gaming experience. Players expect a seamless experience, and even minor delays can lead to frustration. Understanding the causes of lag and implementing strategies to mitigate it is vital.

Understanding Lag

Lag refers to the delay between a player's input and the game's response. This can manifest in various forms, including frame rate drops, input delay, or network latency. It is essential to identify the source of lag to implement effective solutions.

Common Causes of Lag:

1. **Frame Rate Drops**: When the number of frames rendered per second (FPS) drops below the target (usually 30 or 60 FPS), the game may feel sluggish.
2. **Input Delay**: This can occur if the game takes too long to process player inputs, causing a noticeable delay between action and response.
3. **Network Latency**: In online multiplayer games, lag can be caused by delays in data transmission over the internet.

Techniques to Reduce Lag

1. **Optimize Rendering**: Reduce the number of draw calls, simplify shaders, and lower texture resolutions to improve rendering performance.

- **Batching**: Combine multiple objects into a single draw call to minimize the overhead of rendering.
- **Culling**: Implement frustum culling to avoid rendering objects that are outside the player's view.

1. **Use Efficient Algorithms**: Optimize algorithms used for physics calculations, AI behavior, and other game mechanics.

- **Spatial Partitioning**: Use techniques such as Quad-trees or Octrees to manage large numbers of objects efficiently.
- **Simplified Physics**: Use simpler collision shapes (e.g., bounding boxes instead of complex meshes) to reduce the computational load.

1. **Profile Performance**: Regularly profile your game to identify bottlenecks in performance. Utilize profiling tools provided by your game engine (like Unity Profiler or Unreal Insights) to track CPU and GPU usage.

2. **Reduce Memory Usage**: Excessive memory usage can lead to lag due to frequent garbage collection. Optimize memory allocation by:

- **Object Pooling**: Reuse objects instead of frequently creating and destroying them to minimize memory fragmentation.
- **Optimize Asset Loading**: Load assets asynchronously to prevent blocking the main thread.

1. **Adjust Quality Settings**: Allow players to adjust graphical settings according to their hardware capabilities. Providing options for reducing shadows, textures, and effects can help maintain a stable frame rate.

Increasing Frame Rate

Achieving a high frame rate is critical for delivering a smooth gaming experience. Frame rates above 60 FPS are often desirable, particularly in fast-paced games.

Strategies to Increase Frame Rate:

1. **Resolution Scaling**: Dynamically adjust the game's resolution based on performance metrics. Lower the resolution during intense moments to maintain frame rates, and increase it during calmer moments.
2. **Use of LOD Models**: Implement Level of Detail (LOD) models for objects to reduce the polygon count based on distance from the camera.
3. **Optimize Animation**: Use techniques such as animation blending and bone-based animation to reduce the overhead associated with rendering complex animations.
4. **Efficient Asset Management**: Minimize the number of unique textures and materials to reduce state changes and draw calls.
5. **Implement Frame Rate Cap**: Capping the frame rate can stabilize performance. For example, capping at 60 FPS can help maintain consistent performance across different hardware configurations.

Level of Detail (LOD) Techniques

Level of Detail (LOD) techniques are crucial for optimizing graphics in 3D games. By dynamically adjusting the complexity of 3D models based on their distance from the camera, developers can maintain high frame rates without sacrificing visual fidelity.

Understanding LOD

LOD refers to the practice of using multiple models of varying detail levels for the same object. When an object is far away from the camera, a less detailed model is used, while a more detailed model is rendered when the object is closer. This technique reduces the overall rendering load, allowing for more complex scenes without significantly impacting performance.

Implementing LOD

1. **Creating LOD Models**: Create several versions of each model, varying the number of polygons. For example, a character might have a high-resolution version for close-ups, a medium-resolution version for mid-range views, and a low-resolution version for distant views.
2. **Distance Thresholds**: Define distance thresholds for when to switch between LOD models. Use a simple formula based on the camera's distance from the object to determine which model to render.
3. **Automatic LOD Generation**: Many 3D modeling tools and game engines offer features for automatically generating LOD models, saving time and effort during the development process.
4. **Performance Testing**: Regularly test and profile performance while implementing LOD techniques to ensure they are effectively reducing the rendering load without introducing visual artifacts.

Visual Considerations

While LOD is essential for performance, it's also crucial to ensure that the transition between LOD models is seamless and does not disrupt the visual experience.

1. **Crossfade Transitions**: Implement crossfade transitions between LOD models to smooth out the visual changes as the camera moves.
2. **Adaptive LOD**: Consider implementing adaptive LOD techniques that dynamically adjust based on the player's frame rate and performance metrics. For example, if frame rates drop below a certain threshold, the game can automatically switch to lower LOD models.
3. **Testing Visual Quality**: Regularly test your game to ensure that LOD transitions do not negatively impact the overall visual quality. Player feedback can be invaluable in identifying areas for improvement.

Memory Management and Performance Profiling

Effective memory management is critical for optimizing game performance. Poor memory usage can lead to crashes, slow load times, and increased lag, ultimately frustrating players.

Understanding Memory Management

Memory management involves allocating, using, and freeing memory effectively. In games, this includes managing textures, models, audio assets, and other resources.

Key Concepts in Memory Management:

1. **Static vs. Dynamic Allocation**: Understand the difference between static and dynamic memory allocation. Static allocation reserves memory at compile time, while dynamic allocation occurs at runtime.
2. **Garbage Collection**: Familiarize yourself with how garbage collection

works in your chosen language and game engine. For example, languages like C# (in Unity) handle garbage collection automatically, while C++ requires manual memory management.

3. **Memory Footprint**: Monitor the memory footprint of your game to ensure it stays within reasonable limits. Excessive memory usage can lead to lag and crashes.

Strategies for Effective Memory Management

1. **Resource Management**: Load and unload assets as needed. Use asset bundles or streaming techniques to manage resources dynamically, loading them into memory only when required.

2. **Pooling Resources**: Implement object pooling for frequently used objects, such as bullets or particles. This reduces the overhead of creating and destroying objects and minimizes memory fragmentation.

3. **Reduce Texture Sizes**: Use compressed texture formats to minimize memory usage. Balance visual quality with memory requirements, particularly for mobile and lower-end devices.

4. **Memory Profiling Tools**: Utilize memory profiling tools available in your game engine (e.g., Unity Profiler, Unreal Memory Profiler) to monitor memory usage in real time and identify memory leaks or excessive allocations.

Performance Profiling

Performance profiling is essential for identifying bottlenecks in your game. By analyzing performance data, developers can pinpoint areas that require optimization and ensure the game runs smoothly.

1. **Frame Rate Profiling**: Use profiling tools to monitor frame rates across different hardware configurations. Identify the most demanding scenes and optimize accordingly.

2. **CPU and GPU Profiling**: Analyze CPU and GPU usage to determine

where performance issues arise. Optimize code and rendering processes to reduce overhead.

3. **Testing on Target Platforms**: Regularly test your game on target platforms (PC, mobile, console) to ensure it performs well across all devices. Each platform may have unique performance characteristics that need to be addressed.

4. **Player Feedback**: Gather player feedback during beta testing phases to identify performance issues that may not be apparent in your development environment.

Tips for Optimizing for Different Platforms (PC, Mobile, Console)

Each platform has unique performance characteristics and limitations. Understanding these differences is crucial for optimizing your game effectively.

PC Optimization

1. **Graphics Settings**: Allow players to customize graphics settings based on their hardware. Provide options for texture quality, anti-aliasing, shadows, and particle effects.

2. **Multi-threading**: Take advantage of multi-core processors by implementing multi-threading for background tasks such as AI calculations and physics simulations.

3. **High-Resolution Textures**: PCs can handle higher resolution textures, but ensure that they are used judiciously to avoid excessive memory usage.

4. **Support for VR and High-FPS**: If developing for VR or aiming for high frame rates, optimize rendering and input handling to minimize latency and provide a smooth experience.

Mobile Optimization

1. **Resource Management**: Mobile devices have limited memory and processing power. Optimize textures, models, and audio assets to reduce memory usage and improve performance.
2. **Battery Consumption**: Minimize battery consumption by reducing CPU and GPU workloads. Implement options to lower graphics settings and limit background processes.
3. **Touch Controls**: Optimize touch controls for responsiveness. Ensure that the game runs smoothly at varying frame rates to accommodate different devices.
4. **Performance Testing**: Test on a variety of mobile devices with different specifications to identify and address performance issues specific to each device.

Console Optimization

1. **Hardware Constraints**: Consoles have fixed hardware configurations, making it essential to optimize for specific hardware. Utilize platform-specific features and tools provided by the console manufacturers.
2. **Memory Management**: Consoles typically have limited memory compared to PCs. Optimize memory usage, particularly for textures and assets, to fit within these constraints.
3. **Asset Streaming**: Implement asset streaming techniques to load levels and assets seamlessly without disrupting gameplay.
4. **Use of Console Features**: Take advantage of console features such as achievements, trophies, and social integrations to enhance player engagement.

In this chapter, we explored various techniques and strategies for optimizing game performance, including reducing lag, increasing frame rates, implementing Level of Detail (LOD) techniques, managing memory effectively, and optimizing for different platforms. As you continue your journey in game development, keep these optimization strategies in mind to create smooth, engaging, and enjoyable gaming experiences.

The journey of game optimization is ongoing, as each project presents its unique challenges. Regularly profiling performance, testing on target platforms, and gathering player feedback will help you refine your optimization strategies and ensure your game delivers the best possible experience. In the following chapters, we will delve deeper into advanced topics and empower you with the knowledge to take your game development skills to new heights.

Chapter 17: Testing Your 3D Game

Testing is an essential phase in the game development process that can make or break the success of a game. The objective is not only to identify and fix bugs but also to ensure that the game delivers a fun, engaging experience. This chapter explores the importance of playtesting, the debugging tools and techniques available, methods for gathering player feedback, and how to iterate on game design based on testing results.

Importance of Playtesting

Playtesting is the process of having real players play your game to evaluate its mechanics, design, and overall enjoyment. It provides invaluable insights that developers cannot achieve through self-testing alone. The goal is to observe how players interact with the game and gather feedback to refine and improve it.

Benefits of Playtesting

1. **Identify Issues Early**: Playtesting allows developers to spot problems in gameplay mechanics, level design, and user interface before the game is released. Early identification can save time and resources.
2. **Understand Player Behavior**: Observing how players navigate and interact with the game helps developers understand player expectations and preferences. This can lead to more intuitive design choices.
3. **Enhance Gameplay Experience**: Feedback from playtesters can

reveal what elements of the game are enjoyable and which ones may need adjustments, leading to a more engaging overall experience.

4. **Test Balance and Difficulty**: Playtesting helps assess the game's difficulty curve. Developers can fine-tune the challenge level to keep players engaged without becoming frustrated or bored.

5. **Foster Community Involvement**: Engaging players in the testing process can create a sense of community and investment in the game. Players often feel more connected to a game that they helped shape.

Types of Playtesting

1. **Alpha Testing**: This initial phase typically involves a small group of internal testers, including developers, friends, and family. The focus is on identifying major bugs and gameplay issues.

2. **Beta Testing**: This phase includes a larger group of external testers who provide feedback on a nearly finished product. Beta testing focuses on polishing the game and ensuring it meets player expectations.

3. **Closed and Open Testing**: Closed testing involves a limited number of players with controlled access, while open testing allows anyone interested to participate, providing a broader range of feedback.

4. **Remote Testing**: In today's digital age, remote playtesting has become increasingly popular. Testers can play from their own devices while developers observe their interactions through screen-sharing or recording software.

Conducting Playtests

To conduct effective playtests, developers should:

- **Define Objectives**: Determine what specific aspects of the game you want to test, such as mechanics, levels, or user interface.
- **Recruit Testers**: Find players who represent your target audience. Consider a diverse group to gather varied perspectives.

- **Create a Testing Environment**: Ensure that the testing environment is conducive to focus and free from distractions. Provide necessary hardware and software setups.
- **Prepare Instructions**: Give clear instructions to testers about what you want them to focus on and how to provide feedback.
- **Observe and Record**: Monitor the playtest sessions and take notes on player behavior, struggles, and feedback.

Debugging Tools and Techniques

Debugging is a crucial part of game development, allowing developers to identify and resolve issues that arise during testing. Effective debugging tools and techniques can streamline this process, making it easier to deliver a polished final product.

Debugging Tools

1. **Integrated Development Environment (IDE) Debuggers**: Most game engines come with built-in debuggers that allow developers to pause the game, inspect variables, and step through code line by line. Examples include Visual Studio for C# in Unity or the built-in debugger in Unreal Engine.
2. **Performance Profilers**: Profiling tools help identify performance bottlenecks by analyzing CPU and GPU usage, memory allocation, and frame rates. Tools like Unity Profiler and Unreal Insights provide visual representations of performance data.
3. **Error Logging**: Implementing logging systems can help capture runtime errors and exceptions. Logs can be invaluable for diagnosing issues that players encounter.
4. **Unit Testing Frameworks**: Unit testing involves writing tests for individual functions and components to ensure they work as intended. Frameworks like NUnit for C# or Jest for JavaScript can help catch issues early in development.

5. **Visual Debugging Tools**: Some engines offer visual debugging tools that display object positions, collisions, and other visual information in real time. This can help quickly identify graphical glitches or physics-related issues.

Debugging Techniques

1. **Reproduce the Issue**: One of the first steps in debugging is reproducing the problem. Understand the conditions under which the bug occurs to narrow down potential causes.
2. **Divide and Conquer**: Isolate the section of code or the feature causing the issue. Commenting out sections of code can help identify where the problem lies.
3. **Incremental Testing**: Regularly test new features in small increments to identify issues early. This technique helps prevent accumulating a backlog of bugs to address later.
4. **Peer Reviews**: Collaborate with other developers for code reviews. Fresh eyes can spot potential issues or offer alternative solutions that may not have been considered.
5. **Use Assertions**: Implement assertions in your code to catch errors and enforce assumptions. Assertions help ensure that conditions are met during runtime, aiding in early detection of issues.

Gathering Feedback from Players

Collecting feedback from playtesters is essential for refining the game. Effective feedback mechanisms can provide developers with clear insights into player experiences and preferences.

Methods for Gathering Feedback

1. **Surveys and Questionnaires**: After playtesting sessions, provide testers with surveys or questionnaires that ask specific questions about their experience. Use a mix of multiple-choice and open-ended questions for comprehensive feedback.

2. **Observation and Interviews**: Conduct direct observations during playtesting sessions and follow up with interviews. Engaging in conversations with players can provide deeper insights into their thoughts and feelings about the game.

3. **Feedback Forms**: Create feedback forms that players can fill out immediately after testing. Keep them concise to encourage completion, and focus on key aspects of the game.

4. **Focus Groups**: Organize focus group discussions with a select group of playtesters. These discussions can yield qualitative insights and foster discussion about the game's strengths and weaknesses.

5. **In-Game Feedback Mechanisms**: Consider integrating feedback mechanisms directly into the game. For example, players can rate levels or features at the end of gameplay sessions.

Analyzing Feedback

1. **Categorize Feedback**: Sort feedback into categories such as gameplay mechanics, graphics, sound, and user interface. This organization helps identify common themes and prioritize areas for improvement.

2. **Identify Trends**: Look for patterns in feedback from multiple testers. If several players mention similar issues, it's likely an area that requires attention.

3. **Prioritize Changes**: Not all feedback will be actionable. Prioritize changes based on the severity of the issue and the potential impact on the overall game experience.

4. **Maintain an Open Dialogue**: Stay engaged with your playtesting community. Updating testers on how their feedback has influenced

the game fosters goodwill and encourages continued participation in future testing sessions.

Iterating on Game Design Based on Testing

Game design is an iterative process that relies heavily on feedback from testing. The ability to adapt and improve based on playtest results is crucial for creating a successful game.

The Iteration Process

1. **Review Feedback**: After gathering feedback, review it thoroughly with your development team. Discuss which elements resonated with players and which did not.
2. **Define Changes**: Identify specific changes that will enhance the game. This could range from adjusting difficulty levels to redesigning certain mechanics or levels.
3. **Prototype Changes**: For significant changes, create prototypes or mock-ups to test new ideas before full implementation. This allows for quick iteration and evaluation.
4. **Implement Changes**: Once you have a clear plan, implement the changes into the game. Ensure that all team members are aligned on the new direction and understand their roles in the process.
5. **Retest the Game**: After implementing changes, conduct another round of playtesting to evaluate the impact of your adjustments. Continue this cycle of feedback and iteration to refine the game further.

Embracing Failure

In game development, not every idea will work out as planned. Embrace failure as a part of the process and learn from it. When playtesters express dissatisfaction, analyze the feedback constructively and explore alternative solutions.

1. **Conduct Post-Mortems**: After major testing phases, hold post-mortem discussions to analyze what went well and what didn't. This reflection helps identify effective practices and areas for improvement in future iterations.
2. **Maintain Flexibility**: Be willing to pivot your design approach based on feedback. Remaining flexible and open to new ideas is essential for creating a game that resonates with players.
3. **Iterate on Design Principles**: As you iterate on game design, revisit fundamental design principles. Ensure that changes align with your core vision for the game while also meeting player expectations.

Testing your 3D game is a critical component of the development process that significantly impacts the final product. By prioritizing playtesting, utilizing effective debugging tools and techniques, gathering meaningful player feedback, and iterating on design based on testing results, developers can create engaging and polished gaming experiences.

As you move forward in your game development journey, remember that testing is an ongoing process. Each stage of development presents new challenges and opportunities for refinement. By fostering a culture of continuous improvement, embracing player input, and remaining flexible in your approach, you can craft games that captivate and entertain players. In the upcoming chapters, we will explore more advanced topics to further enhance your game development skills and empower you to create memorable gaming experiences.

Chapter 18: Preparing for Release

As the development phase of your 3D game comes to an end, the focus shifts to preparing for its release. This chapter outlines the critical steps necessary to ensure your game is packaged, marketed, and legally compliant before it reaches players. Each of these components is essential to the successful launch of your game, ultimately determining its reception and longevity in a competitive market.

Packaging and Exporting Your Game

Understanding Game Packaging

Packaging your game refers to the process of preparing it for distribution. This involves compiling all game assets, code, and resources into a format suitable for the platform on which you intend to release it. Proper packaging ensures that your game functions correctly and provides a seamless experience for players upon installation.

Steps for Packaging Your Game

1. **Organize Your Project Files**

- Before packaging your game, ensure that all files are organized logically. This includes assets such as textures, audio files, scripts, and levels. Keeping your project tidy will not only make packaging easier but also help in future updates and debugging.

1. **Select the Right Build Configuration**

- Depending on the platform, you may need to configure specific build settings. Most game engines, such as Unity or Unreal Engine, provide options for different build types (development, testing, or production). Choose the production configuration to ensure optimal performance and that debugging information is excluded.

1. **Set Up Asset Compression**

- Large game files can lead to longer download times and storage issues for players. Utilize asset compression to reduce file sizes without significantly impacting quality. This can include compressing textures, audio files, and other assets. Most game engines have built-in tools to handle this.

1. **Testing Your Build**

- Before finalizing your package, conduct thorough testing. This includes playing through the entire game, checking for bugs, and ensuring that all assets load correctly. Testing should cover various hardware configurations and operating systems if applicable.

1. **Create the Installation Package**

- Once the build is tested and finalized, create an installation package. Depending on the platform, this might involve creating an executable (.exe) file for Windows, an app bundle for macOS, or an APK for Android. Ensure that the installation process is straightforward for users.

1. **Documentation and User Guides**

- Prepare documentation that explains how to install and play your game. This can include system requirements, installation steps, and troubleshooting tips. Providing clear documentation enhances the user experience and can reduce the number of support requests.

Exporting Your Game to Various Platforms

1. **Exporting for PC**

- For Windows, macOS, or Linux, ensure that you test the installation process on all targeted operating systems. Package your game as an installer or a zip file, and include a README file with necessary instructions and information.

1. **Exporting for Consoles**

- If you plan to release your game on consoles like PlayStation, Xbox, or Nintendo Switch, be aware that each platform has specific requirements and processes. This often includes adhering to certification processes and guidelines set by the console manufacturers.

1. **Exporting for Mobile**

- For mobile platforms such as iOS and Android, consider screen resolutions and control schemes. Create separate builds for different devices to optimize performance. Additionally, adhere to platform-specific guidelines regarding app submission, such as Apple's App Store Review Guidelines or Google Play's Developer Policy.

1. **Cloud Gaming and Streaming Services**

- With the rise of cloud gaming platforms, consider preparing your game for distribution on services like Google Stadia or NVIDIA GeForce

NOW. This may involve additional optimization and adaptations for streaming technology.

Final Checklist Before Release

- Ensure all assets are included and correctly referenced.
- Test the installation process on various devices and platforms.
- Verify that performance metrics meet or exceed expectations.
- Create and organize all necessary documentation for players.
- Prepare marketing materials, including screenshots and trailers.

Legal Considerations: Copyrights and Licenses

Understanding Copyrights

Copyright is a legal protection that grants creators exclusive rights to their work. This includes the ability to reproduce, distribute, and display their creations. In the gaming industry, copyright covers various elements, including code, artwork, music, and narrative.

1. **Registering Your Copyright**

- While copyright protection is automatic upon the creation of a work, registering your copyright can provide legal advantages, such as the ability to sue for infringement and statutory damages. In the United States, you can register your copyright with the U.S. Copyright Office.

1. **Protecting Your Game Assets**

- Ensure that all original content, such as artwork, music, and scripts, is protected under copyright law. Keep records of creation dates and any licensing agreements for assets that may have been obtained from third-party sources.

Licenses and Agreements

1. **Third-Party Assets**

- If you use third-party assets (e.g., music, graphics, or code snippets), ensure that you have the appropriate licenses to use them in your game. This may involve purchasing licenses or adhering to specific usage guidelines set by the asset creators.

1. **End User License Agreement (EULA)**

- A EULA is a legal agreement between you and the players that outlines how they can use your game. This document typically covers terms of use, restrictions, and liability. Having a well-drafted EULA can protect your rights and set clear expectations for players.

1. **Terms of Service**

- If your game includes online features or a community aspect, consider creating a Terms of Service document. This outlines the rules for using your game and can help mitigate potential issues related to user behavior or content moderation.

Trademarks and Branding

1. **Registering Trademarks**

- Consider registering trademarks for your game title, logo, and any unique branding elements. Trademarks provide legal protection against unauthorized use and help establish your brand identity in the marketplace.

1. **Brand Consistency**

- Maintain consistency in your branding across all marketing materials, social media, and in-game assets. This helps build recognition and trust among your players.

Marketing Your Game: Trailers, Screenshots, and Websites

The Importance of Marketing

Marketing is crucial to the success of your game. It helps create buzz, attracts potential players, and establishes a connection between your game and its audience. A well-executed marketing strategy can significantly enhance your game's visibility and sales.

Creating Engaging Trailers

1. **Elements of a Good Trailer**

- A compelling game trailer should showcase the game's unique features, gameplay mechanics, and story elements. Focus on visual storytelling and capture the essence of your game in a short, engaging video (typically 1-3 minutes long).

1. **Highlight Key Features**

- Include snippets of gameplay that highlight exciting moments, special abilities, or unique environments. Use dynamic editing to maintain viewer interest and provide a clear sense of what players can expect.

1. **Utilize Sound and Music**

- Incorporate sound effects and music that align with your game's theme. High-quality audio can significantly enhance the emotional impact of your trailer.

1. **Call to Action**

- End your trailer with a strong call to action, encouraging viewers to wishlist the game, visit your website, or follow your social media accounts for updates.

Captivating Screenshots

1. **Choosing the Right Screenshots**

- Select screenshots that represent the most visually appealing aspects of your game. These could include stunning landscapes, action sequences, or engaging character designs.

1. **Image Quality**

- Ensure all screenshots are high resolution and properly framed. Avoid cluttered images; focus on clear compositions that highlight the game's strengths.

1. **Descriptive Captions**

- Accompany screenshots with descriptive captions that provide context and intrigue. This helps convey the story or mechanics behind what players are seeing.

Building an Engaging Website

1. **Website as a Hub**

- Your website should serve as the central hub for all information related to your game. Include sections for news, trailers, screenshots, and a blog to keep players updated on development progress.

1. **SEO Optimization**

- Implement search engine optimization (SEO) strategies to improve your website's visibility. Use relevant keywords in titles, descriptions, and content to attract potential players through organic searches.

1. **Email Sign-Ups**

- Encourage visitors to sign up for a mailing list to receive updates. This can be an effective way to build a community and keep players engaged throughout development and after the game's release.

1. **Social Media Integration**

- Promote your social media accounts prominently on your website. Maintain an active presence on platforms like Twitter, Instagram, and Facebook to engage with your audience and share updates, artwork, and behind-the-scenes content.

Choosing a Platform for Release: Steam, App Stores, etc.

Popular Distribution Platforms

1. **Steam**

- Steam is one of the most popular digital distribution platforms for PC games. It offers extensive features, including community forums, achievements, and mod support. To release your game on Steam, you'll need to go through the Steam Direct process, which includes a submission fee and approval process.

1. **Epic Games Store**

- Epic Games Store is another growing platform that has gained popularity due to its favorable revenue sharing model for developers. It also provides marketing support and promotional opportunities for released games.

1. **Console Platforms**

- For console releases (e.g., PlayStation, Xbox, Nintendo Switch), developers typically need to partner with the respective platform holders. This often involves a certification process, which can include rigorous testing and adherence to specific guidelines.

1. **Mobile App Stores**

- For mobile games, the primary platforms are the Apple App Store and Google Play Store. Each has its own submission process and guidelines that developers must follow, including considerations for in-app purchases, advertisements, and privacy policies.

1. **Itch.io**

- Itch.io is an indie-focused platform that allows developers to set their own prices and distribution terms. It's an excellent option for smaller games or experimental projects, providing flexibility and direct engagement with your audience.

Factors to Consider When Choosing a Platform

1. **Target Audience**

- Consider where your target audience is most active. Research which platforms are most popular for your game genre and adjust your release strategy accordingly.

1. **Monetization Options**

- Each platform has different revenue sharing models and monetization options. Evaluate which model aligns best with your business strategy, whether it's premium sales, in-app purchases, or subscriptions.

1. **Market Reach**

- Assess the potential market reach of each platform. A platform with a larger user base can offer more exposure, but also comes with higher competition.

1. **Technical Requirements**

- Be mindful of the technical requirements for each platform, including hardware specifications, submission guidelines, and any additional development work needed to comply with platform standards.

Planning Your Release Strategy

1. **Release Date and Timing**

- Choose a release date that considers market trends and competition. Avoid launching alongside major titles unless you have a solid marketing strategy to stand out.

1. **Soft Launch vs. Full Launch**

- Consider a soft launch to test the game in a limited market before a full launch. This allows you to gather feedback and make necessary adjustments before a wider release.

1. **Post-Launch Support**

- Plan for post-launch support, including updates, bug fixes, and community engagement. Players will appreciate ongoing support, which can help build a loyal player base.

1. **Metrics and Analysis**

- After release, track player metrics and feedback to gauge success. Use this data to inform future updates and marketing strategies.

Preparing for the release of your 3D game involves careful planning and execution across various facets, including packaging, legal considerations, marketing, and platform selection. By taking the time to meticulously prepare each aspect of your release, you can maximize your game's potential for success in a competitive market.

With the right marketing strategy, a clear understanding of legal obligations, and a well-packaged game, you'll set the stage for a successful launch. Remember that the work doesn't stop once the game is released; ongoing support and engagement with your player community are key to maintaining interest and enhancing your game's reputation. As you embark on this exciting phase of your game development journey, embrace the opportunities and challenges that lie ahead, and prepare to share your creation with the world.

Chapter 19: Case Studies in 3D Game Development

As the 3D gaming landscape continues to evolve, understanding the successes and challenges faced by popular titles and indie developers provides invaluable insights into effective game design, marketing strategies, and player engagement. In this chapter, we'll conduct a comprehensive analysis of some of the most successful 3D games, examine lessons learned from indie developers, and scrutinize the game design choices that have contributed to their success.

Breakdown of Popular 3D Games

1. Minecraft

Overview Released in 2011 by Mojang Studios, Minecraft has become one of the most iconic games of all time, renowned for its unique blocky graphics and sandbox gameplay. Players can explore, build, and create their worlds, giving them a level of freedom rarely seen in gaming.

Game Design Choices

- **Sandbox Mechanics:** Minecraft's open-world structure allows players to approach the game however they wish. This flexibility caters to various playstyles, from exploration to creation and survival.
- **Procedural Generation:** The use of procedural generation creates vast,

diverse landscapes, ensuring that no two worlds are the same. This feature encourages exploration and discovery, keeping players engaged for long periods.

- **Modular Gameplay:** The game is built around simple building blocks, making it accessible for players of all ages. The core mechanics are easy to grasp, but the complexity comes from the combinations and possibilities of these blocks.

Lessons Learned

- **Community Engagement:** Minecraft has thrived on community involvement. The introduction of modding capabilities and user-generated content has fostered a vibrant community that contributes to the game's longevity.
- **Updates and Expansions:** Regular updates have kept the game fresh and relevant, introducing new features, biomes, and mechanics that enhance gameplay without changing its core identity.

2. Fortnite

Overview Epic Games' Fortnite, released in 2017, quickly became a cultural phenomenon, blending battle royale gameplay with building mechanics and vibrant art styles. Its success can be attributed to its innovative gameplay, social features, and effective marketing strategies.

Game Design Choices

- **Battle Royale Format:** The 100-player free-for-all format creates high-stakes gameplay, encouraging player engagement and competitiveness. Players can drop into the map, loot weapons, and eliminate opponents to be the last one standing.
- **Building Mechanics:** Fortnite's unique building mechanics set it apart from other battle royale games. Players can quickly construct structures for defense or elevation, adding a layer of strategy to encounters.

- **Seasonal Events:** Fortnite regularly introduces themed seasons and events that alter the game world, keeping content fresh and engaging. These events often tie in with popular culture, drawing in players from diverse backgrounds.

Lessons Learned

- **Cross-Platform Play:** By supporting cross-platform play, Fortnite enables friends to play together regardless of the device, significantly broadening its player base.
- **Emphasis on Community and Social Interaction:** The game promotes social engagement through features like in-game concerts, challenges, and community events, making it a social platform beyond just a gaming experience.

3. The Legend of Zelda: Breath of the Wild

Overview Released in 2017 by Nintendo, Breath of the Wild redefined open-world gaming with its emphasis on exploration and environmental storytelling. It garnered critical acclaim for its innovative mechanics and breathtaking visuals.

Game Design Choices

- **Open-World Exploration:** Players can tackle objectives in any order, encouraging exploration and experimentation. The game's vast landscapes are filled with secrets, quests, and unique challenges.
- **Dynamic Physics Engine:** The game features a robust physics engine that allows for creative solutions to puzzles and combat scenarios. Players can manipulate the environment in numerous ways, fostering a sense of agency.
- **Minimal Hand-Holding:** Breath of the Wild avoids excessive tutorials, allowing players to learn through exploration and trial and error. This design choice empowers players to engage with the game world more

deeply.

Lessons Learned

- **Environmental Storytelling:** The game effectively uses its environment to convey narrative elements, encouraging players to piece together the story through exploration rather than relying solely on dialogue or cutscenes.
- **Player Agency:** Empowering players to make choices and solve problems creatively leads to a more rewarding gameplay experience.

4. Overwatch

Overview Blizzard Entertainment's Overwatch, released in 2016, is a team-based first-person shooter that emphasizes cooperation and diverse character abilities. It has garnered a dedicated player base and competitive scene.

Game Design Choices

- **Hero-Based Gameplay:** Overwatch features a diverse cast of characters, each with unique abilities and roles. This variety allows players to find characters that match their playstyle and fosters teamwork.
- **Objective-Based Maps:** The game's maps are designed around specific objectives, encouraging players to work together rather than simply eliminate opponents. This design choice promotes strategic gameplay.
- **Regular Updates and Events:** Blizzard frequently introduces new characters, maps, and seasonal events, keeping the game fresh and maintaining player interest.

Lessons Learned

- **Character Diversity:** Providing a wide range of characters with different abilities ensures that players can find their niche, promoting a more inclusive gaming experience.

- **Focus on Teamwork:** Designing gameplay around cooperation encourages players to develop strategies and work together, enhancing social interaction and player engagement.

Lessons from Indie Game Developers

Case Study: Hollow Knight

Overview Developed by Team Cherry, Hollow Knight is a critically acclaimed indie game that blends elements of platforming, exploration, and combat. Released in 2017, it quickly gained a loyal following due to its stunning art style and deep gameplay mechanics.

Key Takeaways

- **Art and Aesthetics:** Hollow Knight's hand-drawn art style and atmospheric soundtrack create an immersive experience that captivates players. Indie developers can prioritize artistic vision and design even with limited resources.
- **Depth Over Breadth:** The game focuses on delivering a polished experience with rich lore and challenging gameplay rather than overwhelming players with content. This approach fosters player engagement and encourages exploration.
- **Community Engagement:** Team Cherry engaged with the community through updates and expansions, listening to player feedback to improve the game and expand its content.

Case Study: Stardew Valley

Overview Stardew Valley, developed by Eric Barone (ConcernedApe), is a farming simulation game that gained immense popularity since its release in 2016. It combines farming, crafting, and social interaction in a charming pixel art world.

Key Takeaways

- **Player Freedom:** The game offers players the freedom to pursue various activities at their own pace, appealing to a broad audience. This flexibility enhances player satisfaction and replayability.
- **Nostalgic Appeal:** By drawing inspiration from classic farming games like Harvest Moon, Stardew Valley taps into nostalgia while innovating with new mechanics and systems.
- **Community Building:** The emphasis on relationships with non-player characters fosters emotional connections, making players invested in the game's world.

Case Study: Celeste

Overview Celeste, developed by Maddy Makes Games, is a platformer released in 2018 that combines challenging gameplay with a heartfelt narrative. It focuses on the journey of a young woman climbing a mountain while facing her inner struggles.

Key Takeaways

- **Narrative Integration:** The game weaves its narrative into the gameplay, allowing players to connect emotionally with the protagonist. This integration enhances the overall experience and motivates players to progress.
- **Accessibility Features:** Celeste includes various accessibility options, ensuring that players of all skill levels can enjoy the game. This commitment to inclusivity sets a positive example for other developers.
- **Challenging Yet Fair:** The game's design philosophy emphasizes challenge without frustration. The checkpoint system allows players to retry difficult sections quickly, promoting a sense of achievement.

Analyzing Game Design Choices in Successful 3D Games

1. User Experience and Interface Design

Intuitive Controls Successful games prioritize intuitive controls that allow players to focus on the gameplay rather than struggling with the interface. For instance, games like Overwatch and Fortnite utilize simple, easily customizable control schemes, enabling players to adapt quickly.

Feedback Mechanisms Clear feedback is essential in keeping players engaged. Visual and audio cues, such as sound effects for collecting items or notifications for completing objectives, help players understand their progress and actions in the game.

Accessibility Options Incorporating accessibility options can significantly enhance player engagement. Games like Celeste and The Last of Us Part II have set benchmarks for including features that accommodate players with varying abilities, ensuring that no one is excluded from the gaming experience.

2. Balancing Challenge and Reward

Difficulty Curves Successful games often employ well-structured difficulty curves, gradually increasing challenges as players improve their skills. For example, Hollow Knight introduces challenging mechanics progressively, ensuring that players are adequately prepared for tougher battles.

Reward Systems Implementing reward systems that provide players with meaningful incentives keeps them motivated. Games like Destiny 2 and Fortnite utilize loot boxes, unlockable content, and experience points to reward players for their efforts and achievements.

Failure and Persistence Games that encourage persistence through failure foster a growth mindset in players. Titles like Dark Souls and Celeste embrace challenging gameplay, allowing players to learn from their mistakes and improve over time.

3. World-Building and Narrative Integration

Environmental Storytelling Games like Breath of the Wild and Dark Souls excel in environmental storytelling, allowing players to discover the narrative through exploration and interactions with the world. This method encourages players to engage more deeply with the lore and history of the game.

Character Development Well-developed characters enhance the narrative experience. Games like The Witcher 3 and Life is Strange provide players with emotionally rich narratives, drawing them into the story and making them care about the characters' journeys.

Choice and Consequence Games that incorporate meaningful choices and consequences, like Detroit: Become Human or The Walking Dead, create a sense of agency for players, allowing them to influence the story's outcome and feel more connected to their decisions.

4. Innovation and Trendsetting

Breaking Conventions Innovative games often break traditional conventions, setting new trends in the industry. For example, the introduction of battle royale mechanics in PUBG and Fortnite revolutionized multiplayer gaming, leading to a surge of similar titles.

Cross-Genre Blending Games that successfully blend genres, such as the combination of RPG mechanics in Monster Hunter: World, often attract a wider audience. This fusion of gameplay styles creates unique experiences that stand out in a crowded market.

Embracing Technology Developers who embrace emerging technologies, such as virtual reality or augmented reality, can create groundbreaking experiences that redefine gaming. Titles like Beat Saber and Pokémon GO have demonstrated the potential of these technologies to engage players in new ways.

In examining the case studies of popular 3D games and indie developers, we uncover valuable insights that can inform our approach to game design. Understanding the elements that contribute to a game's success—from engaging mechanics and compelling narratives to community involvement and accessibility—can guide aspiring developers as they embark on their own 3D game development journeys.

As we look ahead, it's crucial to recognize that the gaming landscape is continually evolving. By studying successful titles and learning from both industry giants and indie developers, we can craft experiences that resonate with players and stand the test of time. The lessons drawn from these case studies remind us of the importance of creativity, innovation, and player engagement in the dynamic world of 3D game development.

Chapter 20: Beyond the Basics: Advanced Game Development

As the gaming industry evolves, developers must stay ahead of the curve by embracing advanced techniques and technologies. This chapter will delve into key areas of advanced game development, including multiplayer implementation, the integration of virtual reality (VR) and augmented reality (AR), future trends shaping the industry, and resources for ongoing learning and growth in 3D game development. By understanding these advanced concepts, developers can create more immersive and engaging experiences for players.

Implementing Multiplayer in 3D Games

Understanding Multiplayer Game Types

Before diving into the technical aspects of implementing multiplayer functionality, it's crucial to understand the various types of multiplayer games. Multiplayer games can be broadly categorized into several types:

1. **Cooperative Multiplayer:** Players work together to achieve common objectives, often facing challenges that require teamwork. Examples include games like *Left 4 Dead* and *Minecraft*.
2. **Competitive Multiplayer:** Players compete against each other, either directly in player-versus-player (PvP) modes or indirectly through

leaderboards and rankings. Titles like *Fortnite* and *League of Legends* exemplify competitive multiplayer games.

3. **Massively Multiplayer Online Games (MMOs):** These games support large numbers of players interacting within a persistent world. Examples include *World of Warcraft* and *Final Fantasy XIV*.

4. **Asymmetrical Multiplayer:** Different players assume different roles or objectives, creating unique gameplay dynamics. Games like *Dead by Daylight* and *Evolve* fall into this category.

Network Architecture

The backbone of any multiplayer game is its network architecture, which determines how players connect, communicate, and interact with the game world. There are two primary network architectures used in multiplayer game development:

1. **Client-Server Architecture:** In this model, players connect to a central server that hosts the game. The server manages game state, synchronizes player actions, and handles authoritative decisions. This architecture is common in many competitive games due to its stability and security.

- **Pros:** Centralized control, easier to manage game state, enhanced security.
- **Cons:** Server costs, potential latency issues, single point of failure.

1. **Peer-to-Peer (P2P) Architecture:** In a P2P model, players connect directly to each other, sharing game state and interactions without a central server. This architecture can reduce server costs and enhance responsiveness.

- **Pros:** Reduced server costs, potential for lower latency.
- **Cons:** Security concerns, more complex to manage, potential for

inconsistencies in game state.

Synchronization and Latency Compensation

One of the significant challenges in multiplayer game development is ensuring that all players see a consistent view of the game world despite network latency. To address this challenge, developers often implement techniques such as:

1. **State Synchronization:** Regularly sending updates about the game state (e.g., player positions, object interactions) between clients and the server ensures that all players have the same information.
2. **Interpolation and Prediction:** Clients can use interpolation to smooth out movements based on the last known positions of other players. Prediction can also be used to estimate future positions based on velocity and direction, reducing the perceived impact of latency.
3. **Lag Compensation Techniques:** Techniques such as client-side hit detection and rewinding the game state can help mitigate the effects of lag, making the experience smoother for players.

Security and Cheat Prevention

Multiplayer games are often targets for cheating, which can ruin the experience for legitimate players. To combat cheating, developers can implement several security measures:

1. **Server Authority:** By having the server handle critical game logic and validate player actions, developers can reduce the likelihood of cheating. Clients should only send their inputs, and the server should determine the outcome.
2. **Anti-Cheat Systems:** Implementing anti-cheat software can help detect and prevent cheating by monitoring player behavior and identifying anomalies.

3. **Regular Updates:** Frequent updates and patches can help close security loopholes and keep the game environment secure.

Virtual Reality (VR) and Augmented Reality (AR) in 3D Games

Understanding VR and AR

Virtual Reality (VR) and Augmented Reality (AR) are transforming the gaming landscape by providing players with new ways to interact with game worlds. While both technologies immerse players in engaging experiences, they differ fundamentally:

- **Virtual Reality (VR):** VR creates a completely immersive experience by placing players in a digital environment. Players typically wear VR headsets that track their movements, allowing them to interact with the virtual world as if they were physically present.
- **Augmented Reality (AR):** AR overlays digital content onto the real world, allowing players to interact with both physical and virtual elements simultaneously. This technology often utilizes mobile devices, such as smartphones and tablets, to enhance the user experience.

Designing for VR

When designing VR games, developers must consider several key factors to create an immersive and enjoyable experience:

1. **Comfort and Usability:** VR can cause discomfort or motion sickness if not designed carefully. Developers should minimize rapid movements and provide options for players to adjust settings such as movement speed and comfort levels.
2. **Intuitive Controls:** Controls in VR should be intuitive and mimic natural movements. Using motion controllers can enhance player engagement and make interactions feel more realistic.

3. **Spatial Awareness:** Designing game environments that allow players to navigate naturally is crucial. Providing visual cues and landmarks can help players orient themselves within the virtual space.
4. **Audio Design:** 3D spatial audio enhances the immersion of VR experiences. Players should hear sounds as if they originate from specific locations in the game world, creating a more realistic experience.

Designing for AR

AR game development also comes with unique challenges and considerations:

1. **Context Awareness:** AR games should be aware of the player's environment, allowing for dynamic interactions with real-world elements. This requires utilizing sensors and cameras to understand the surroundings.
2. **User Interface Design:** Traditional user interfaces may not translate well to AR. Developers should design interfaces that integrate seamlessly with the physical world, avoiding clutter and distractions.
3. **Gameplay Integration:** AR experiences should blend digital content with real-world activities in meaningful ways. Games like *Pokémon GO* successfully encourage players to explore their surroundings while engaging with virtual characters.

Future Trends in 3D Game Development

As technology continues to advance, several trends are shaping the future of 3D game development:

1. Cloud Gaming

Cloud gaming is gaining traction, allowing players to stream games directly from servers without the need for high-end hardware. This trend democratizes access to gaming, enabling players with lower-spec devices to enjoy high-quality experiences.

2. Artificial Intelligence and Machine Learning

The integration of AI and machine learning in game development is enhancing various aspects, including:

- **Dynamic Content Generation:** AI can create content on the fly, providing players with unique experiences each time they play.
- **Intelligent NPCs:** Machine learning can be used to develop more realistic and adaptive non-player characters, improving player engagement and immersion.

3. Cross-Platform Play

Cross-platform play is becoming increasingly important as players expect to connect with friends regardless of their device. Developers are prioritizing cross-platform compatibility to expand their player bases and enhance social interactions.

4. Enhanced Realism and Graphics

Advancements in graphics technology, such as ray tracing and improved rendering techniques, are pushing the boundaries of realism in games. As hardware becomes more powerful, developers can create stunning visuals that enhance the immersive experience.

5. Game Streaming and Content Creation

The rise of platforms like Twitch and YouTube Gaming has changed how players engage with games. Developers are recognizing the importance of integrating features that support content creation and streaming, such as in-game tools for recording and sharing gameplay.

Resources for Continued Learning

To stay competitive in the ever-evolving field of game development, continuous learning is essential. Here are some valuable resources for developers looking to expand their knowledge and skills:

1. Online Courses and Platforms

- **Coursera and edX:** These platforms offer courses from top universities on game design, programming, and related subjects.
- **Udemy and Pluralsight:** These platforms provide a wide range of courses specifically focused on game development tools, languages, and techniques.

2. Books and Publications

- **"Game Programming Patterns" by Robert Nystrom:** This book covers design patterns and best practices in game development.
- **"The Art of Game Design: A Book of Lenses" by Jesse Schell:** This comprehensive book provides insights into the game design process and creative thinking.

3. Online Communities and Forums

- **GameDev.net:** A popular forum for game developers to discuss ideas, share knowledge, and seek advice.
- **Reddit:** Subreddits like r/gamedev and r/IndieDev are excellent places to connect with fellow developers and share experiences.

4. Game Development Tools and Documentation

- **Unity and Unreal Engine:** Both engines have extensive documentation, tutorials, and community support to help developers learn and master their tools.
- **GitHub:** Exploring open-source projects and collaborating with other developers can provide valuable hands-on experience and exposure to different coding styles.

5. Conferences and Events

- **GDC (Game Developers Conference):** One of the largest gatherings of game developers, offering sessions, workshops, and networking opportunities.
- **PAX and IndieCade:** These events celebrate indie games and provide a platform for developers to showcase their work while networking with industry professionals.

In this chapter, we explored advanced game development topics, including multiplayer implementation, the integration of VR and AR technologies, future trends shaping the industry, and valuable resources for continued learning. By embracing these advanced concepts, developers can create more engaging and immersive experiences, positioning themselves at the forefront of the evolving gaming landscape.

As technology advances, the opportunities for innovation in game development are limitless. By staying informed and adapting to new trends and tools, developers can push the boundaries of what is possible in 3D gaming, crafting experiences that captivate and inspire players around the world.

Appendix

I n the world of 3D game development, understanding the terminology, troubleshooting common issues, and having access to code samples and tutorials can significantly enhance your learning experience. This appendix serves as a valuable resource for both novice and experienced developers. It includes a comprehensive glossary of terms frequently used in game development, troubleshooting tips for common issues, and a collection of code samples and additional tutorials to aid your projects.

Glossary of Terms

3D Graphics Terms

- **3D Model:** A mathematical representation of a three-dimensional object. Models can be created using various software tools and are made up of vertices, edges, and faces.
- **Texture Mapping:** The process of applying a 2D image (texture) to a 3D model's surface to give it detail and realism.
- **Shader:** A program that tells the computer how to render an object's surface, including its color, brightness, and texture. Shaders are essential for achieving realistic lighting and material effects.
- **Vertex:** A point in 3D space defined by its coordinates (X, Y, Z). Vertices are the building blocks of 3D models.
- **Normal Map:** A texture used to simulate bumps and wrinkles on a surface without increasing the polygon count of the model.

Game Development Terms

- **Game Engine:** A software platform that provides the tools and features necessary to create and develop games. Popular engines include Unity, Unreal Engine, and Godot.
- **Game Loop:** The cycle that keeps the game running. It processes user input, updates the game state, and renders the game frame repeatedly.
- **Collision Detection:** The process of determining when two objects in the game world intersect or come into contact. This is crucial for gameplay mechanics like character movement and interactions.
- **Animation Rig:** A system of bones and controls that allows a 3D model to be animated. Rigs define how a character moves and poses.
- **Artificial Intelligence (AI):** The simulation of human intelligence processes by machines. In games, AI governs the behavior of non-player characters (NPCs).

Programming Terms

- **Script:** A set of instructions written in a programming language that tells the game engine how to perform specific tasks or behaviors.
- **API (Application Programming Interface):** A set of functions and procedures that allows different software components to communicate with each other.
- **Debugging:** The process of identifying and removing errors or bugs from code to ensure proper functionality.
- **Framework:** A platform for developing software applications. In game development, frameworks provide pre-built components that simplify the development process.
- **Event System:** A programming paradigm that allows the game to respond to user inputs and other events. It facilitates interaction between different components of the game.

Game Design Terms

- **Level Design:** The process of creating the environment, challenges, and gameplay elements in a game. It involves designing maps, puzzles, and the overall flow of the game.
- **Game Mechanics:** The rules and systems that govern how players interact with the game. This includes controls, scoring systems, and player objectives.
- **User Interface (UI):** The means through which the player interacts with the game, including menus, HUD (heads-up display), and buttons.
- **Playtesting:** The practice of testing a game with real players to gather feedback and identify areas for improvement.
- **Game Narrative:** The story and plot elements that drive the game. This includes character development, dialogue, and lore.

Troubleshooting Common Issues

As with any software development, you may encounter issues during your 3D game development journey. Below are common problems and their troubleshooting solutions.

1. Performance Issues

Problem: The game runs slowly or has a low frame rate.
Solution:

- **Optimize Assets:** Reduce the polygon count of 3D models and use lower-resolution textures where possible. Consider using Level of Detail (LOD) techniques to manage performance.
- **Adjust Lighting Settings:** Use baked lighting instead of dynamic lighting when possible to reduce processing load.
- **Profile the Game:** Utilize profiling tools provided by your game engine to identify performance bottlenecks and optimize the code accordingly.

2. Collision Detection Problems

Problem: Objects pass through each other or do not collide as expected.
Solution:

- **Check Colliders:** Ensure that colliders are properly set up on both objects. Adjust their sizes and positions as needed.
- **Layer Management:** Use layers to define which objects should interact with each other. Ensure the collision settings are configured correctly in the physics engine.
- **Continuous Collision Detection:** For fast-moving objects, enable continuous collision detection to prevent them from passing through other objects.

3. Animation Issues

Problem: Characters do not animate correctly or have odd movements.
Solution:

- **Check Animation Rig:** Ensure that the character's rig is properly set up and that all bones are correctly weighted.
- **Animation Transitions:** Review the transitions between animations to ensure they blend smoothly. Adjust the animation curves if necessary.
- **Update Animation States:** Make sure that the correct animation states are being triggered in response to game events.

4. Input Handling Issues

Problem: Player inputs are not registering or behaving incorrectly.
Solution:

- **Input Mapping:** Verify that the input mappings are correctly configured in the game engine. Check if keys or controller buttons are mapped to the correct actions.

- **Debug Input Code:** Use debug statements to check if input events are being registered in your code. This will help identify any issues with input handling logic.
- **Test on Different Devices:** If the issue persists, test the game on various devices to see if it's a hardware-specific problem.

5. Sound Problems

Problem: Sounds do not play or are out of sync with events.
Solution:

- **Check Audio Sources:** Ensure that audio sources are properly attached to game objects and that the audio files are correctly imported into the project.
- **Adjust Audio Settings:** Review the audio settings in the game engine, including volume levels and spatial audio settings.
- **Debug Sound Events:** Use debug logs to verify that sound events are being triggered at the appropriate times in the game.

Code Samples and Additional Tutorials

This section provides a selection of useful code samples and links to additional tutorials that can enhance your understanding of 3D game development.

Code Samples

1. Basic Character Movement (C# in Unity)
   This code snippet demonstrates how to implement basic character movement in Unity using the CharacterController component.

```csharp
using UnityEngine;

public class PlayerMovement : MonoBehaviour
{
    public float speed = 5f;
    private CharacterController controller;

    void Start()
    {
        controller = GetComponent<CharacterController>();
    }

    void Update()
    {
        float moveX = Input.GetAxis("Horizontal");
        float moveZ = Input.GetAxis("Vertical");
        Vector3 move = transform.right * moveX +
        transform.forward * moveZ;
        controller.Move(move * speed * Time.deltaTime);
    }
}
```

2. Basic Jumping Logic (JavaScript in Three.js)

In this example, we implement a simple jumping mechanic in a Three.js-based game.

```javascript
let isJumping = false;
const jumpHeight = 5;

function update() {
    if (isJumping) {
        player.position.y += jumpHeight * deltaTime; // deltaTime
        is the time elapsed since the last frame
        if (player.position.y >= originalY + jumpHeight) {
```

```
        isJumping = false; // Stop jumping when reaching the
        peak
    }
} else if (player.position.y > originalY) {
    player.position.y -= jumpHeight * deltaTime; // Simulate
    falling
}

// Input handling for jumping
if (input.jump && !isJumping && player.position.y ===
originalY) {
    isJumping = true;
}
}
}
```

3. Simple AI Behavior (C# in Unity)

This code sample outlines a basic AI behavior for an enemy that patrols between two points.

```csharp
csharp
Copy code
using UnityEngine;

public class EnemyPatrol : MonoBehaviour
{
    public Transform pointA;
    public Transform pointB;
    public float speed = 2f;
    private Vector3 target;

    void Start()
    {
        target = pointA.position;
    }

    void Update()
    {
        MoveTowardsTarget();
```

```
    CheckForArrival();
}

void MoveTowardsTarget()
{
    transform.position =
    Vector3.MoveTowards(transform.position, target, speed *
    Time.deltaTime);
}

void CheckForArrival()
{
    if (Vector3.Distance(transform.position, target) < 0.1f)
    {
        target = target == pointA.position ? pointB.position
        : pointA.position;
    }
}
}
```

Additional Tutorials

- **Unity Learn:** Unity Learn offers a wealth of tutorials covering everything from the basics to advanced topics in Unity development.
- **Unreal Engine Documentation:** Unreal Engine Docs provides comprehensive guides and tutorials for learning Unreal Engine.
- **Three.js Fundamentals:** Three.js Fundamentals offers tutorials and resources specifically for 3D graphics development using Three.js.
- **Blender Tutorials:** Blender Guru is an excellent resource for learning Blender, including modeling and animation techniques.
- **GameDev.net:** GameDev.net is a community-driven site where developers can find articles, forums, and resources related to all aspects of game development.

Conclusion of the Appendix

This appendix is designed to be a practical resource for developers at all levels. Whether you are encountering common issues or seeking to expand your knowledge with code samples and tutorials, the information provided here aims to support your journey in 3D game development. As you continue to learn and create, remember that the game development community is vast and filled with resources to help you succeed. Happy coding!

www.ingramcontent.com/pod-product-compliance
Lightning Source LLC
Chambersburg PA
CBHW071243050326
40690CB00011B/2243